BUDGETING

FOR BEGINNERS

The How to Guide to Budgeting Become Debt
Free Fast and Save Money

(Easy Ways You Can Learn How to Budget Your
Money)

William Gonzalez

Published by Alex Howard

William Gonzalez

All Rights Reserved

Budgeting for Beginners: The How to Guide to Budgeting Become Debt Free Fast and Save Money (Easy Ways You Can Learn How to Budget Your Money)

ISBN 978-1-77485-065-7

Legal & Disclaimer

The information contained in this book is not designed to replace or take the place of any form of medicine or professional medical advice. The information in this book has been provided for educational and entertainment purposes only.

The information contained in this book has been compiled from sources deemed reliable, and it is accurate to the best of the Author's knowledge; however, the Author cannot guarantee its accuracy and validity and cannot be held liable for any errors or omissions. Changes are periodically made to this book. You must consult your doctor or get professional medical advice before using any of the suggested remedies, techniques, or information in this book.

Table of Contents

Introduction

This book contains proven steps and strategies on how to efficiently manage your money.

It does not matter if you earn a million dollars a month. If you do not know how to manage your money, you will lose it all. Without budgeting, your money will always be in danger of being spent on whimsical purchases.

This book teaches the basics of budgeting that should have been taught to us all in schools. It also touches on the topic of investing your money to make it grow. We start with your goals for budgeting and saving money. We then discuss the strategies and tools that you will need to create and implement a sustainable plan. If you follow the tips in this book, you will reach your financial goals fast through budgeting. You may even become a millionaire.

Thanks again for downloading this book, I hope you enjoy it!

Chapter 1: Budgeting Basics

It can be said that the hardest part about living on a budget is sticking to it. We always have the best of intentions when we create a personal or household budget but is "actually following the budget" that is the most difficult part of the whole situation. However, I would argue that forming the habit is the difficult part. After that habit is formed, it can be fairly easy to stick to it.

Know the Definition of A Budget

We don't all know what "living on a budget" entails. When you hear that phrase, what do you instantly think of?

"Having no fun."

"Saving all of your money."

Is that about right?

Create Some Goals

We are all at different parts of our lives. Because of this, we all have different financial obligations. Not only that, we also want different things out of our futures.

Some of us want to be able to retire and travel. Some just want to be able to live in a tiny house. Other people want to be able to have vacations homes that they can visit when they feel the urge to move around. Some of us need to save for our families. Others just want some play money and money to live comfortably in the future.

Ask yourself what you want out of your life. What kinds of short term and long term goals do you have and how do you need to financially ready yourself for those goals? Keep in mind that short terms goals should take no longer than a year to complete while an example of a long term goal would be, "Save for retirement" or "Put away money for my child's education".

Do you need to save a lot of money for a new house? To be ready for children? Or perhaps so you can start your own business. How long will it take for you to save up the necessary funds in order to make these goals attainable?

Remember that these goals aren't set in stone. Things happen in our lives that make us rethink what we want out of our future. You can change around the items on this list as you grow older and experience more things. You might want to aim for a promotion now but in five years, you may change that goal to "Start my own small business so I can be my own boss."

When coming up with these goals, consider what makes you happy – not what other people think you should do. This was one of the hardest lessons that I had to learn. While I was making my goals, I chose to pursue the goals that my parents chose for me. This meant that I planned (financially) to follow their dreams so I was inevitably unhappy. When

I finally realized how unhappy I was, I found myself in debt and unhappy with the direction that my life was going.

Luckily for me (and a lot of you out there also), it's never too late to follow your own dreams. I set up short term and long term goals and I made that plan. One of those goals was to get myself out of debt and start fresh.

I wrote those goals down, plastered them in places that spent a lot of time in (the corkboard in my office and on my kitchen fridge). This ensured that I had reminders on a daily basis. I also made sure to tell the friends and family that I trusted the most. They helped hold me accountable to those goals.

When I wanted to frivolously spend some money, my friends would ask me if it was within my budget (normally I would end up putting the item back for something different). I can happily say that I am now debt free and following my passions.

Pay Close Attention To Your Net Income

One of the biggest pitfalls when it comes to planning out and living to a budget is creating and following a plan that is within your income. In a time where material possessions have become something of a status symbol, we have learned to live outside our means. This is one of the main reasons why a lot of people are in credit card debt and can't stick to a budget or save money.

The first step that you identify how much money you have coming in. Knowing your income is important. Some of you may have to estimate how much you have coming in every month because you own your own business, run a freelance or by-contract business, or because your income fluctuates.

If this is you, make sure that you underestimate how much income you bring in each month. I only suggest this because it is easy to overestimate and that will cause your budget to be unreasonable and unattainable.

Also remember to take into account your employer deductions for taxes, retirement plan, insurance, Social Security, and maybe spending account allocations.

When You Create Your Plan

When you create your budget plan - and you've found your average monthly income – divide your income into two big categories: fixed spending and variable expenses.

The expenses that would fit under fixed spending would include your utilities and bills that don't change much each month. This would include your mortgage, car payments, credit card payments, regular utilities, etc.

The items that would fit under variable expenses includes expenses that change every month: entertainment, food (though this can fit in either depending on your habits), gas and travel expenses, etc.

I suggest that you record these expenses for a couple months to see what your trends and habits fall. If you are anxious to get a budget plan ready, I suggest that you look into your bank records. Online banking has made things incredibly easy these days. Some online banking accounts even break down your spending for you depending on where you shop.

My online bank account does that exact thing; they organize my spending habits by categories. This makes it much easier to keep track of where my money goes.

At the minimum, I would manually break up your spending into three different categories:

Needs and necessities

Savings

Desires

Needs include the fixed and variable costs that are necessary to living a healthy life. The savings section would include both emergency funds and retirement. The desires section would cover everything else.

Now it is time to personalize your budget.

Okay, so you've analyzed your spending habits. Now it's time to personalize a budget. A great thing that is simultaneously obnoxious is the fact that every budget should be personalized. This means that you don't have to be pigeonholed into keeping a budget that doesn't fit your needs (Yay!). However, this also means that you have to work harder to come up with the perfect budget that does (Ohh...).

Okay, now that you've figured out what your fixed spending number is, set that aside every month so that you will always have that money available for important expenses. What you have left should be divided up into variable items. This number is also a variable in and of itself. If you allot a certain amount on things like clothes but you know that you need to save for a TV, you can skim a little from your clothes fund and add that to your TV fund.

Making Your Budget.

Creating your actual budget can be done in as little as four steps after you've done all of that prep work.

Keep a record of your spending and analyze your results. Record your spending and have your significant other record theirs as well. I suggest keeping a small notebook and pen with you at all times for one month. In addition to that, keep a spreadsheet on your computer. Transcribe your

Plan for your next month's spending. If you live with a significant other, make sure that you plan together and that you take all of your expenses into consideration, even if you both have separate bank accounts. You don't have to keep track of each other's "desired" sections, however it is important to come up with a spending cap. When you want to buy something of a certain amount — which will differ with each couple — you may want to defer with each other. Some of you may not need to do this. Others feel that it is a courtesy to one another. While others yet feel that it is necessary because you have joint accounts. My husband and I keep our own records for small spending. However, if something costs $100 or more, we mention it to each other. If something costs $500 or more, we discuss it as a team so that we can come up with rational and smart choices.

Look for ways that you can spend less. While spending a little bit for a long time can add up, so can saving a lot of money. Saving just a little bit over a long period of time can add up to some incredible savings. To do this, consider some of these options:

Shop at a cheaper grocery store

Buy generic brands

Cook at home instead of eating out

Entertain at your house instead of going out to a club or movie

Utilize coupons during sales

You can also find ways to boost your income. If you have a hobby or talent, you may be able to use it to earn some extra money. Teaching your hobby to others can prove to be profitable. You can also sell your wares on an online shop, or at local markets. One great bonus is that you may be able to turn this side job into a full time job if you ever lose your main source of income. Handy, huh?

Check Your Spending Habits On A Monthly Basis

Are you sticking to your budget? If not, where are you going astray and how can you fix that? Take a look at your spending every month and compare it to your personal budget worksheet to see how things are going. If you find that you're often going over-budget in some areas out of necessity, you should consider cutting elsewhere to keep things under control.

Chapter 2: Effects Of The Compound Effect On Savings

Undoubtedly, you have heard that you should start saving early. This chapter will look at why this advice is so important and how the compound effect works on a savings plan established early in your life.

This chapter is a direct continuation of the previous one. Chapter 1 introduces the compound effect in simplistic terms, with a couple of abstract examples. This chapter will advance your education and provide great financial tips that illustrate the benefits of starting saving early. This time though, we shall use examples that heavily involve money.

More time means more accumulation and a stronger influence of the compound effect

Ask any person who keeps a close eye on the markets to give you a sound bite on a factor that draws the most positive market effects. Chances are that he or she will bring up long-term investment as a sure way to make big money. If the person is in the mood for further education, he or she will explain that long-term investment is only possible if the investments occur on a regular basis, and follow a clear cut, disciplined plan.

Transfer this mentality from investment to saving.

The longer you have been saving up amounts, the more money you will naturally have in your reserves. Even more importantly, there will be more of an amount for the compound effect to work on every passing month. Regardless of whether you are actually investing or just saving up money in the bank, even a small money amount has the capacity to grow exponentially.

As a young person making the first steps in the workforce, take advantage of any existing employer-sponsored plan. If there is none, begin saving immediately into a personal retirement account such as a Roth IRA.

Selecting an Investment Vehicle Ideal for You: The Low-Cost Index Fund

When you are selecting an investment vehicle, you should deeply consider diversification and expenses. As a young person, you may not have as much money to work with as the older folk, at least at first, so you have to tread carefully.

A great starting point would be a low cost index fund. An index fund refers to a type of mutual fund that has a portfolio, which is built to track or match components of a market index. The most popular example of a market index is Standard & Poor's (S&P's) 500 Index. An index fund provides wide market exposure, low costs of operation, and an appealingly low portfolio turnover.

These funds usually adhere to preset standards—an example is efficient tax planning rules. These rules stay static irrespective of the state of the market. For instance, an index fund modeled on Standard & Poor's 500 index exposes you to U.S.'s 500 biggest companies.

As your fund grows, you can add extra index funds for some diversity. In your diversification endeavors, you can opt for small cap funds and international index funds. This resource page will take you to an article that thoroughly covers the index fund phenomenon:

Understanding the Potency of the Compound Effect

To help us understand the importance of having the compound effect working for you, let us calculate a few hypothetical returns:

The Standard and Poor (S&P500) has, on a 30 year period average, returned 11%. You could extend the 30-year period to 40 and the average still sits at 11%. Let us say you are 25 years old and have decided to start your retirement plan ASAP. If you were to go ahead and put away $1,200 every year into an S&P 500 modelled index fund, and this index fund maintained the 11% S&P 500 return:

You would have successfully accumulated about $775,000 by the time you reached the retirement age of 65.

If you were to retire at 55, the amount accrued, with the same contribution in place, would be $265,000. If you were to retire at 45 years, you would have $80,000.

If for some odd reason, you were to retire at 35, you would only have saved up $22,000. By the way, the expense ratio for an index fund is really low—like 20 basis points/0.20% or less. Still, it should factor in despite its minimal effect in the general scheme of things.

The points above give you an idea of how compounding interest works, and why the time involved is very important in regards to how it influences your money. The picture painted is a compelling one. Nevertheless, this book is determined to give you the full picture without glossing over anything, so here goes:

While the S&P 500 has indeed given 11% returns on average for the past 40 years or so, it has not done quite so well of late. In the last 2 decades, the average has been closer to 9%. Over the last decade, the average sits at 7%. Of course, when we use round numbers like 11% or 9%, it is for the sake of illustration. There are decimal figures on top of the round numbers.

Let us use a return figure that is closer to the average of the last few years. 8% is an ideal number. If we use the same $1,200 contribution, we will get the following results:

In 40 years, you will have accumulated $335,000

In 30 years, you will have accumulated $146,000

In 20 years, you will have accumulated $59,000

In 10 years, you will have accumulated $18,000

The amounts above may have diminished significantly compared to the previous ones, but they tell the story just as successfully. By this point, you know the compounding effect is an absolute force: the figures do not lie. However, what is the underlying takeaway when you look at the accumulated amounts, with the 10 year spells separating each?

The takeaway is that time is very important. He who starts earliest ends up in the best place. Taking the latter example, the fellow who begins saving up as early as 25 and retires at 65 will have more than double the money accumulated, compared to the one who starts saving at 35. This is assuming a similar contribution every year.

To ensure you have enough money to invest so as to enjoy the power of the compound effect, let's discuss some effective strategies that you can follow to attain greater financial control and save more.

Chapter 3: Setting Up A Budget For The First Time

When you are setting up a budget for the first time, you ideally will want to have a place where you can record the money that is going in and out of your financial accounts and also a list of your expenses and your monthly payment due for each one.

Tools Needed:

Spreadsheet Software OR notebook, pen and calculator (if no spreadsheet is available)

List of Expenses, Bills and Debts

Access to your current bank account statement (online or paper statements if applicable)

To set up your budget you will need make three (3) major columns either in the spreadsheet software or notebook you will be using. The three columns will have the following headings:

List of Expenses/Revenue, Day of the Month it is Due, Budget Month:

List of Expenses	Day Due	January	February
Rent	1st	$400	
Electricity	1st	100	
Water	1st	75	
Car Payment	15th	50	
Credit Card #1	23rd	25	
Total		$650	
List of Revenue	Day Due	January	February

Salary Paycheck #1	1st	$1000	
Salary Paycheck #2	15th	$1000	
Total		$2000	
Net Profit/Net Loss		$1,350	

You will want to make sure that when you are creating columns for the budget months, you will have enough columns for all 12 months for the year. Ideally, the minimum number of columns you will have is 14, one for every month of the year, the day when the expenses or income occurs, and the list of income and expenses.

Under the different month columns you will want to put how much you will have to pay for those expenses. For credit cards and other debts that have a minimum monthly payment due, you want to put that amount. We'll explain why later.

For non-minimum payment debts that have costs that are variable such as utilities, you will want to put the most your bill payment has. The reasoning behind this is if you put the most you have ever paid in any given month, the assumption is that your payment will always be that same amount or less.

In the cells designated for column totals, you can manually total the amounts with a calculator or you can use the formula used to calculate a group of numbers. This is called the SUM formula.

The formula goes like this: =SUM(C2:C6). SUM means you want the spreadsheet to do an addition calculation. C2 and C6 can be exchanged for the first cell in that column with an expense # in it and C6 is the very last cell in that column.

For this example, I want to use the January Column so the formula will be =SUM(C2:C6), math wise it will be =SUM(all number starting from $400 through $25) which should end up $650 in the example above.

Then you will want to do the same for the bottom half of those same columns, in the income section of your spreadsheet. You will want to put in what your typical salary will be or the income you have coming in, what dates and the lowest amount you typically get. You want to put the lowest amount you typically get because you want to plan for worst case scenarios.

As you get your income coming in, you can change those numbers to reflect the actual amounts but when projecting ahead of time, you want to plan for worst case scenario and put in the smallest amount you've ever had coming in and you wanted to use the same SUM formula using the cells where your income amounts are listed to calculate your total salary for that given month.

In the cells designated for the Net Profit/Loss amounts, you want to calculate how much you have left over after you pay your expenses. You can use the subtraction formula which is =X-Y where X is the cell that has the total income amount and you subtract Y which is the cell that has the total expenses amount in that column. In the aforementioned example it is =X-Y which translates into =$1000 - $650. When the formula totals it should be $1,350.

When you first create a budget spreadsheet, you can use the numbers in the aforementioned example until you get the hang of using formulas in the spreadsheet software. Then you can revise it with numbers in your specific situation.

Once you finish your spreadsheet, then you can look at it more in-depth and see how your monthly financial situation will end up. As you find out your exact bill payments due and your income amounts coming in, then you can change the assumed numbers to the actual numbers to get a more realistic view of your financial outlook.

Chapter 4: Why Budget - Importance Of Having A Budget

Why is it important to have a budget. In a previous chapter, I mentioned briefly why it is imperative to budget. In this chapter, we will go into depth about why it is important to budget.

You learn to spend only what you have

Thanks to the advent of credit cards, now far too many people have discovered that they can still spend money even when they're broke. Did you know that in 2019, for instance, the average credit card debt for every household was $7,104, a very worrying statistic indeed?

Before the invention of credit cards, people used to live within their means. After earning a salary at the end of the month, you had to pay your bills, and whatever little was left was put in a savings account. Nowadays, many people are abusing and overusing their credit cards only to realize later that their over-expenditure has plunged them into an almost endless pit of debt.

However, if you learn to create and stick to a budget, you are unlikely to find yourself spending more than you have. When you have a budget, you will know your exact earnings per month, how much you can spend, where you need to re-allocate your finances, and how much you will put into savings.

Also, the amazing thing about having a budget is that, creating a budget and sticking to it is also the first step to achieving financial freedom. When you come up with a budget, you start to become more conscious about your spending habits and learn to take a moment to evaluate your spending decisions rather than just spending without taking a moment to analyze your expenditure. The more you do this, the more you are likely to find yourself spending money on things that are not as important to you.

Note: Credit cards are important when used well in helping you build your credit. However, you should not make a habit of using credit cards.

Helps you address poor spending habits

Coming up with a budget helps shed light on your spending habits and enables you to take control of your money. Only when you come up with a proper budget will you discover that all along you have been spending money on the wrong things or those that you don't need. For instance, you may find that you keep buying new clothes every weekend, and somehow you never get to wear those clothes because it was more of an impulse purchase rather than clothes that you wanted.

Budgeting can also help you notice some areas or items that you have been spending too much money on. For instance, eating out for lunch every day may not feel like a big issue at the moment. But if you sit down and add up the cost of eating lunch out almost every day, you'll discover that it is those seemingly small expenditures that amount to over-spending.

Budgeting, therefore, is important if you want to take a closer look at your daily spending habits as it will make you recognize the impact of seemingly insignificant bills to take control of your spending. You should often ask yourself whether what you are about to spend your money on is a necessity to determine its benefit or cost to you. This will prompt you to rethink how you spend money and help you refocus your financial objectives and goals moving forward.

Emergencies will find you prepared

Life is full of moments of uncertainties and unanticipated surprises. You could be happy this very moment only to be hit with news of a tragedy in the family, get injured or ill, or get laid off. These scenarios, among others, can lead to severe financial turmoil. For some reason, it also seems like these surprises always

happen at the worst possible moments –
when you're short of money, hence the
importance of having an emergency fund.

As you come up with a budget, it is critical
to start working on having an emergency
fund that should be made up of no less
than 3 to 6 months of living expenditure.
These surplus funds will keep you from
spiraling into the depths of debt after
riding through the waves of a calamity.

It takes time, sacrifice, and patience to
gather 3 to 6 months' worth of emergency
money, and you cannot achieve that when
you do not have a budget and are just
winging it and going with the flow.

Taking the time to create a budget enables
you to evaluate your expenditures
critically, cut money on things that you do
not need, yet you spend money on to re-
direct that money to your savings. In no
time, if you have self-discipline, you should
have your emergency set-up.

Enables you to be flexible

Most people think that when you set up a budget, it is set on stone, and you cannot change anything. Remember, the budget is meant to work for you. A budget gives you a clear picture of your earnings and expenses. Over the month, you may find that you had allocated more money on something that you now realize that you don't use much of or do not even need. This realization will enable you to transfer money between categories if the need arises throughout the month.

Achieve Financial contentment

Financial contentment is one of the many foundational elements that foster good financial behavior. It holds you back from spending beyond your means, and this will help you enjoy a stress-free life.

If you spend most of your time concentrating on the wealth of other people, you will never be content with what you have. This comparison is what people commonly refer to as "keeping up with the Jones," and it is an awful and financially risky way to live. What you need to do instead is concentrate on your own life, your finances, and how you choose to spend money. And this is where a budget comes in.

The moment you pick your pen to create, tabulate, log, refine or assess everyday expenditure into your budget, you have immediately made a conscious effort to concentrate on what you have instead of what the other person has. You learn to work with what you have and make what you have work, and you are likely to achieve great satisfaction.

Improved Productivity

Did you know that being stressed about money is more likely to get you fired? Poor financial choices can not only ruin your personal life, but it can also hurt your career. In fact, a study by the US Navy discovered that Navy Service members going through financial problems cost the Navy between $172 - $258 worth of productivity every year. What's more, since 1995, job absenteeism due to financial stress has increased by more than 300%. If financial stress is beginning to damage your career, it is time you work on a budget.

Relieves stress and improves happiness and health

Financial problems are a key cause of stress for many people. You already know that poor spending habits can add up to hundreds of dollars per month and thousands annually compounded by interest and could plunge you into debt. This kind of stress caused by debt and other financial problems has been shown to break families, make you lose your job, and even lead to illnesses.

If you have experienced financial stress before, then you've felt how depressing and painful it can be. You work hard and put in extra shifts to earn more, but things only keep getting worse. Already as it were, you can barely keep up this month, and you don't know how long this will last.

You even avoid some essential products or services because you feel they're too expensive; this is no way to live.

And it doesn't end there. The problems spill over to family and friends. Your friends turn into enemies because you can't pay up what you owe, or you've become a burden to them. You're constantly fighting with your spouse because poorly managed finances have driven a wedge between your family and relationship. Why not avoid all this by creating a budget to gain control over your life and your happiness?

As you have learned, creating a budget and sticking to it streamlines your finances, enabling you to live a happier, less stressful life.

Enables you to realize your dreams

Having a budget created to meet your financial goals will make it easier to achieve those goals. If you don't have a budget, don't know much about your expenditures, and spend money on every shiny, pretty object that captures your attention, you will never be able to achieve your financial goals

You need to realize that if you desire to build wealth and achieve financial freedom in the future, you need to take some steps now to ensure this, and this begins by understanding your expenditures, apportioning your finances and saving and investing. For example, if you love to travel and would love to see the world but are unable to do that because you never seem to have enough money, then understanding your expenditure will enable you to re-allocate your finances and save for that trip.

The goal of budgeting is enabling you to come up with your goals, whatever those may be, and working with the income you have to achieve those goals. Remember, you can never achieve anything if you don't even know what you want in the first place.

You can live happily in retirement

A budget can help you build investment contributions and enable you to live comfortably in the future. If you set aside a portion of your funds every month to contribute to your retirement fund such as the 401(k) or IRA, you will ultimately build your 'nest egg'.

However, to achieve this, you will need to sacrifice a bit now while you are productive but the benefits will become more evident a few years down the line. After all, would it not be better that you spend your days in retirement taking trips to beautiful islands or golfing rather than working so hard when you don't even have the energy?

Let us now learn about the different budgeting approaches you can adopt.

Chapter 5: Common Questions Pertaining To Budgeting

The word budgeting is often misunderstood by a huge percentage of the common populace outside of those who are in some way related to, or work in the finance field. However, this is something, that knowingly or unknowingly every man with a remote interest in saving his hard earned coins does at some level or the other. A decent knowledge about the core principles of budgeting will help you immensely in managing your finances.

In this chapter I shall list out some of the most common queries with respect to the concept of budgeting, which will aid you setting targets for the month, earmarking funds, paying off any debts or installments and managing the mortgage without it adversely affecting your liquidity.

What is the ideal amount to be marked for investments?

When it comes to ascertaining the amount of money to be set aside for investment, three factors are of paramount importance. They are age, disposable income and liquidity position. So let us take a look at all three of these, one by one.

☐ As you can imagine, the budgeting decisions and consequent investment tactics depend a lot on the age of the investor. In case of young people, the major factors to be considered include the future investment plans such as real estate purchases or buying residential spaces such as apartments etc. Since at the beginning of careers, the income may not be that high, the amount of money that can be put aside for these purposes will also be less.

☐ The next factor is disposable income. Essentially it is the amount that is left with you after meeting all the pressing needs and requirements in life. In an ideal scenario, it denotes the money that you have in hand after you have spent enough to pay all the bills and other unavoidable expenses. However there is a cache here. This disposable income can either be put away as savings for a rainy day, or it can be spent in acquiring the finer things in life by indulging in some luxuries.

☐Liquidity position denotes the ease or viability of converting your non-cash assets into cash. This is highly important in terms of quantum of the proposed investment. It may be your own money, but if it blocked in some kind of set-up in which you are not allowed to access it before a certain period of time, then you are practically left without that money during such period of time.

One of the most convenient methods of saving up include going in for employer sponsored retirement accounts. These methods allow you to make use of pre-tax money for funding the investment. In this vein, let us answer one of the most frequently asked questions regarding investment; how much of the income to be invested! There is no steadfast answer for this, but a minimum of 10% of your net income will prove to be a tidy sum. Anything higher is always welcome as long as it doesn't leave you high and dry.

How much money should be kept aside for repayment?

The amount of money that should be kept aside of repayment of already existing loans depends to a large extent on the repayment schedule. There are some instruments that can be repaid only in accordance with the terms prescribed and then there are rolling debt instruments that let you pay them off based on your capabilities. Credit cards usually fall into the latter category.

But financial advisors and investment experts hold strong to one maxim here; that is to never invest money in taxable accounts when you have outstanding credit card balances. This is simply because of the reason that most credit card companies charge you anything between 5% and 30% as the annual interest rate, which is pretty much what you can hope to earn from the said investment. Hence it is always advisable to pay off one's dues before earmarking funds for investment in taxable accounts.

When it comes to repayment itself, some research can actually help you a lot here. Some credit agencies will be willing to alter the payment schedules if you request them to do so. Because many a time, we can see people who will be perfectly willing to pay more monthly, but will be tied down by the pre-decided terms and hence end up paying more as interest. In such cases, you can check whether it is possible to have the monthly repayment amount increased. But exercise caution while doing so, because there is something called "prepayment penalties" that may be attracted for repayment of a debt earlier than decided.

What about overpaying the mortgage?

The mortgage is another area where you can employ the method mentioned in the earlier section; that is overpaying. We do agree that in almost all normal cases, the mortgage will be the cheapest source of debt. But still if you can afford to pay more monthly, then very well do so.

But there are some prerequisites that have to be considered here. First and foremost, make sure that all high interest debt is settled completely before you decide to overpay the mortgage. Secondly, ensure that a security net is in place before you take this leap. By security net, what I meant is the creation of an emergency fund worth 2 or 3 months income. Another thing to keep in mind is that there should be no opportunity cost for the amount overpaid. That is, if you had not paid the extra, then the amount should only have gone to savings.

How to chalk out a budget and maintain it?

Preparation and maintenance of a budget is really no rocket science. Do it a few times and you will get the hang of it pretty well. But there are some key pointers to be kept in mind. During the first few months, the stress should be on reviewing the financial statements to ascertain how much money was spent under different heads of expenses. These actual figures should be compared against the figures that you had marked out in the budget. Accordingly the budget should be tweaked.

And then there is the issue of one-time expenses that will invariably crop up every now and then. These include expenses incurred for replacing some major part of your car or any appliance at home etc. It would be prudential to list these under some miscellaneous category instead of regular maintenance expenses, as these are by no means recurring.

You can also get your partner or spouse to prepare one in order to have company. A sibling will also do and the two of you can remind each other to prepare the monthly budget on time. Although most people prefer to prepare one at the beginning of the month, you can do yours at the end as well to remain prepared for the next month.

How to deal with expenses that don't fit anywhere?

As I had mentioned earlier, there will always be expenses that apparently do not fit under any head. Do not worry because this is the case with every budget. By now you must have realized that no budget is perfect and the process of budgeting itself is an ever-evolving, ever-correcting one.

Expenses that cannot be bought under any fixed or variable head should be mentioned under the miscellaneous head. The only thing to be ensured is that, at no point of time should your miscellaneous section show a huge figure as compared to the rest of the budget. This calls for recurrent and timely evaluation of your budget in order to keep it updated and equipped to deal with the varying nature of your finances. Remember, these expenses need to be regular ones and not

something that come about once in a
while. As long as it is a regular expense,
you can add it under the miscellaneous
heading.

Chapter 6: Maintaining A Regular Budget

Changing your habits

In maintaining a regular budget, it is important to develop new spending habits. When you change your bad habits, you will see positive changes in your finances as well. You may need to get rid from a habit like smoking and other vices. You only need to be flexible towards adjustments so that you will be able to maintain a good management of your money.

Be mindful of your spending habits and always know where your money goes. Identify any expensive luxuries you enjoy and try to adjust them or cut them out entirely. Reduce the frequency of other self-treat activities like weekly massage, vacations, going to a salon or buying an expensive wine. You can do these things once or twice a month so that you can add up more money to your savings. Also, you can save money by eating at home more often rather than always going out to eat.

These adjustments will be difficult to do at first and may cause you to feel restricted. Just remember that if you have developed these good habits in spending, you will not only save a lot of money but you will also have better and bigger opportunities to enjoy your earnings. You will have great investments and will be able to afford nicer vacations.

Budget planner

Aside from having a budget record in your computer, you can also print your budget planner so that you can have a hard copy of it in case of emergencies. Before you go to the supermarket or department store, always check your budget to be reminded of the amount of money that should be spent. By constantly checking your budget plan, you can always monitor your spending and can prevent mistakes.

You can also redo or update your budget for at least every 3 months especially when there are significant changes in your income and expenditures. Once you are already comfortable with a certain budget plan, you can stick to it or update it less frequently.

Family cooperation

In maintaining an effective budget, family cooperation is very important. A good budget plan will not have a good effect if the family members are not taking responsibility to stick to it. Set goals that everyone agrees. All members should participate to make the budgeting goals successful. Family meeting and discussions can be helpful in checking your progress and making some necessary adjustments.

Dividing the tasks like organizing a shopping list, making a record of expenses, and software management among family members will help you work as a team. Blaming, arguments and misunderstanding are avoided once everyone understands the purpose of having a budget.

Plan for Emergency and Occasional Expenses

Have a plan for other expenses that may occur anytime like medical expenses, car insurance, celebrations, and family vacations. If you were able to save enough money for it, you can easily provide for these things as they happen. Christmas celebrations, weddings and birthdays are some of the events that may occur. You should at least make a plan on how to cope up with them.

Also, leave room in your budget for some fun stuff. Reward yourself for some time with delicious foods, a concert, or a vacation. Use your savings to give your family an opportunity to enjoy and experience the benefits of your hard work in budgeting. It is not a bad thing as long as it does not affect your financial goals and obligations.

Correct your mistakes

Everyone may encounter mistakes in planning a budget and this is normal. When this occurs, take an action to correct it right away. This is where you learn and discover how to improve your strategies and techniques. Forgive yourself and start again. Be patient and you will surely find an effective budget plan as you continue the process.

Chapter 7: Make Money

Boost your income in your spare time and help pay off those debts quicker. These methods (probably) won't make you rich, but they will help you in the short term. Some ventures begin as side hustles and can cascade into a full-time job and in some cases six-figure salary. Life is about taking your chances, being bold and making your money work for you. One of these ideas alone might not make you much money, but if you pick two or three non-time-consuming ideas, then you could supplement your income nicely. Choose things you can already do rather than trying to learn new skills, as this could cost you time and time is money.

Just like when you are trying to save money, be mindful and remember what you are doing this for — your financial stability and to live a better life.

There are plenty of ways to make money in the short term, and these are just some examples that I have used or people I know have used, when in doubt, get onto the internet to try and find some inspiration. Maybe you have had an idea, and you never got around to applying it, now might be a good time to try it out.

Remember, anytime you make money you might be liable also to pay tax on what you earn. Make sure you pay whatever you owe in a timely and correct way to avoid being fined or hit with a bill at an inconvenient time.

Sell unwanted items − If you have a collection of clothes building up that you don't want or need, get them on eBay. Collectors' items such as old bicycles or sports memorabilia and children's toys also sell well. If you have no use for it or don't wear it anymore then sell it and make some money back. The same goes for CD's, DVD's, games and old games consoles.

Odd jobs – Charge people money to cut lawns, wash cars, walk dogs, clean windows, be a handyman/woman...get creative. If you can do it, then make money doing it.

Online surveys – Various websites offer money (usually not a lot) for you to fill out surveys. It won't take long, and you could bag yourself a little extra income each week.

Search the web – Qmee is a browser add-on which you download onto your computer. It pays you as you go online and browse/shop. Again, you won't get rich doing this, but it is a little extra passively obtained income.

Second job – Get a second job, maybe working evenings if your first job allows. It could be something simple like selling to the neighborhood via a catalog or being a delivery or taxi driver. I wouldn't advocate working a second job for a long amount of time, but if you need the money due to debt, then it should be considered in the short term. Remember, people who get rich do so by having multiple incomes, but they don't tend to get those incomes from working for others.

Student? Sell your books – Student specific books for university and college are notoriously expensive. If you ever had any and put them away, or have just finished with them you should sell them on.

Buy and sell on eBay or Amazon – This really is its own niche. I know of people who have had extensions built onto their houses so that they have enough space to store all of their eBay stock. You really can make a living doing this, but it works well as a side hustle.

There are two ways to do this, you can see what is trending on eBay and try to buy that cheap and sell it for more (think children's playground trends, these tend to be cheap to buy and small which saves you money on postage). You can also bargain hunt, buy cheap and sell expensive. Items like golf clubs and rare vinyl's as well as collector's items can all be found in abundance on eBay. Buy a bargain then sell it on to someone else for more than you paid to make a little profit.

Upcycle and sell furniture – You can buy or take your own old furniture and upcycle it. Taking old furniture and restoring it is nothing new, but restoring it with a modern twist is. Many people now take old tables and chairs, jazz them up with modern colors and patterns then sell them on for a small fortune. If you are really creative you can just offer to be the person who does the restoration and charge others for the job you do without having to source the furniture itself.

Tax rebate – You might be due a tax rebate, and sometimes the tax man doesn't let you know very quickly. Check it out – you could be due a windfall.

Rent out your garage or parking space – You can rent out your disused garage as storage space to other people, and if you live in a city center it might be worth it to rent out your car parking space if you don't need it – check out it out online there are specialized websites made purely for this service.

Ask for a pay rise – Are you a good employee? Do you work hard? Ask for a pay rise then!

Don't just go in to your boss and ask off the bat without any thought though – think of reasons why you deserve a raise, make a list and really think about what sets you aside from other colleagues. Remember though, talk about you, and don't bad mouth others. If your boss agrees then great and if not, you haven't done any harm in asking.

Start a business – If you want to start a fully-fledged business I'm not going to tell you no, it's a great investment if you have seriously thought it through. What I'm suggesting is subtler – many people use local selling pages on social media to sell goods they buy in bulk, you can even set yourself up like a shop and deliver or post items out to people. Use PayPal for safe online transactions and away you go. The future ventures section of the book goes into this in significantly greater detail.

Best rate savings accounts – Don't settle for a savings account with a terrible rate, if your money is sitting idle the least you can do is make sure it is earning half decent interest.

Switch bank accounts – Some bank accounts (in the UK) pay you a cash lump sum when you switch over to them. Might be worth it for the free money!

Wedding dress – Have you got an old wedding dress up in the loft or in the wardrobe? Let's face it; you aren't going to use it again so you might as well sell it on. You can still make good money from old wedding dresses, so it's worthwhile to stick them on eBay and you will be helping someone else have their dream day for less, and we're all about budgeting! Warm fuzzy feelings for everyone.

Get a lodger – If you have a spare room, you could get a lodger. There are various websites set up that arrange this, and you want to make sure you don't take in just anyone off the street. You could charge a couple of hundred pounds (dollars, euros...etc.) a month to your lodger which is not to be overlooked. The UK currently (2017) allows you to rent out a furnished room in your home tax free to the sum of £7,500 a year.

Delayed transport claims – If you have had a flight or a train journey delayed or cancelled you could be in line for a nice little sum of compensation. This is EU regulation so is likely to stop in the UK when they leave the European Union. Various companies offer this service but you can also find blank forms online to use yourself, cutting out the middle man gets you all the compensation.

Drop shipping – A scheme that can work

I came across this simple, but apparently effective idea a few years ago. Quite a few people have made good money doing this, with many earning thousands a month. What's the hitch? It's time consuming and it's a scheme in the truest sense of the word. Let's talk about Drop Shipping.

You can create an Amazon selling page, and on that page, you can sell pretty much whatever you want. Drop shipping is a method of selling items that you do not have nor intend to hold in stock.

You sell the product on one site, in this case it's usually best to use Amazon due to its massive customer base, for more money than you buy that item for off a different supplier. You then have that supplier ship the product directly to the buyer. You don't need space, stock, or employees.

Simple...right?

Except you need to keep on top of how cheap you can buy the item as prices fluctuate, and the customer might decide to return the item, which you have already paid money for, in which case you would have to also return the item and refund the money. In theory, you should never be out of pocket, but cash flow restrictions exist, especially if Amazon doesn't send you any money that is paid to you for several weeks, there is a delay, and you still must buy the item to ship it to your customer as soon as possible. Also, don't forget your supplier might mess up the order; you have no control over this.

I wouldn't say no to this entire but I wouldn't recommend drop shipping either, or any other get rich quick schemes – but I know that some people have made a decent amount of money doing this so I felt I would add this in as an example of what can be achieved, not without risk, but also a warning that these schemes are not always everything they appear.

Don't bite off more than you can chew, if you accept a second job you don't want to burn yourself out. If you end up not being able to work at all or losing your main job due to bad performance you will be in a worse situation. Don't forget to pay any tax owed on that extra income.

There are literally thousands of different ways to make money and a huge number of websites devoted to side hustles. Research methods and ideas, find some that suit you and make some good money.

Do not be fooled into get rich quick schemes, they have drawbacks that may not be advertised with the product of system that could cause you significant financial issues and set you back. Many of these schemes are a way to get other people rich by taking your money – be aware.

Chapter 8: The Great Law Of Wealth Generation- Investments And Assets Acquisition

In the previous chapter, we mentioned that to set aside 10% of your income every month.

Well, the money is not just going to be sitting idle in your account; you must learn how to make that money multiply and generate wealth for you.

To grow the money in your savings account, you need to learn how to invest wisely. You need to send that money out to work for you and yield interests. You also need to protect your principal (the money you invest) in the process. This means distancing yourself from Get-rich-quick schemes, lotteries, gambling and other sensational money making opportunities.

Note: Think of every dollar in your savings account as a soldier who goes out there to capture captives/slaves some of whom you convert to become your soldiers so as to grow your army. The bigger your army is and the more you send the soldiers to battle, the faster your army will grow and the more secure you become.

Principles of Investment

There are so many investment vehicles out there from stocks to mutual funds, real estate and so on and each one has its own unique advantages and disadvantages.

However, there is one principle that you must always follow when you want to invest:

Do not ever invest in anything you do not completely understand.

It doesn't matter whether other people are making millions from it; if you must join the others to make money from it, then you must first make efforts to understand it.

You must completely understand what the investment opportunity is all about, the upsides and downsides of investing in it, what you would do if the investment doesn't turn out as expected and lastly, your exit strategy for when you want to liquidate your investments.

It is important to know all of this before you commit your money to any investment opportunity.

Compound Interest

Always invest in things that will bring you compound interest.

Albert Einstein referred to compound interest as "one of the most powerful forces of the universe". Compound interest is simply accumulated interests on your investments.

For instance, if you invest $100 on a compounding interest basis with an interest rate of 10% per month, after the first month, you would have $110 in your account. By the second month, things start to get a little bit more interesting. You will now earn extra interest of $1 on the interest you earned in the first month. So instead of earning $10 as interest, you earn $11.

If you continue to accumulate the interests and it continues to compound like this over a long period of time, it wouldn't be long before you generate significant wealth from it.

To enjoy the benefits of compound interest however, you must start investing early. If you invest $100 at a compound interest rate of 10% today, after 30 years, you would have a whopping $1,983.74 in your account and would be at a better financial position than someone who only just started investing the same amount with the same interest rate just 10 years ago.

However, it's never too late to start. There's a popular saying that "The best time to plant an oak tree is 100 years ago, the next best time is now".

Here are some tips to keep in mind when investing

Investing Tips

☐**Diversify**

Don't ever put your eggs in one basket. Your investment portfolio should be as diversified as possible. You should have a mix of investment vehicles; some stocks, mutual funds, treasury bills, real estate and so on.

The reason for doing this is to minimize risks and increase profits.

☐Be Focused

Have an investment plan (preferably long term) and stick with it. Don't let the fluctuations in the market sway you. Make sure that any buy or sell decisions you made is made after careful and logical reasoning and not while under a panic attack.

☐Monitor Your Investments

Yes, you can have a fund manager but you must also ensure that you are always aware of what is going on in the market and how your investments are performing.

Lastly, you must have a big heart. Investing involves risk taking and you cannot always be guaranteed of profits at all times. However, if you follow the principles and guidelines set out in this guide, you will be able to minimize losses. You must have a large heart and be able to handle losses well.

The journey to becoming financially free cannot be achieved if you don't put effort as far as debt management is concerned. Let's learn more about debt in the next chapter.

Chapter 9: Budgeting By Month

If you like seeing the big picture you will want to budget by month. Budgeting by month makes sense because most bills are paid on a monthly basis. When you budget by payday you are budgeting for income, but when you are budgeting by month you are budgeting for bills.

Why It Works

Budgeting by month works well for people who have a lot of monthly bills. It is best for people who have more than just rent or utilities to pay each month. People who budget by month probably have credit card payments, loan payments, rent or mortgage payments, car payments and the like. They probably have more luxury bills as well such as cell phone bills and cable or satellite.

When you have a lot of monthly bills it is better to budget by month because you need to see the big picture. It is too difficult to make sure all of your bills are paid by looking at it from a pay period point of view. If you budgeted that many monthly bills by pay period you would be setting aside a dozen small amounts from each paycheck, making your budgeting extremely complicated. The more complicated your budgeting method is, the harder it is to stick to it and be successful.

The Process

In many ways budgeting by month is easier than budgeting by pay period. The first thing you do is calculate your expected income for the month. Include all sources of guaranteed income such as salary and regularly paid child support or alimony. If you have variable income include that as well, but be conservative in your estimates of how much you will earn.

The next thing you need to do is make a list of all of your monthly bills. If you have variable monthly bills such as utilities you should pad these a bit to make sure that you have them covered. It is better to plan to spend more than to not have enough when the time comes to pay your bills.

Then list all of your other expenses such as groceries, household and personal items, and gasoline. You may want to budget luxury expenses as well such as entertainment or dining, vices such as cigarettes, or for gifts.

Make a list of your upcoming large expenditures or things that you are saving for. Decide on an amount you will add to your savings for these things each month. You will want to plan an amount that will be easily met and fit well within your budget without making you strapped.

Add up all of your income and then your expenses. Your expenses should be less than your income. Even if you are just $20 lower than your income, you are doing well. You want to have at least a little bit of leeway in your budget in case something comes up.

This is all there is to your monthly budget. Pretty simple, right? The hard part is making sure you follow your budget.

Gauging Success

It is much harder to stick to a monthly budget. You are probably not being paid monthly. You will have to make sure that you have the money to meet all of your obligations. This means really watching your spending over the course of the month. You will have to split up your bills and pay some out of each pay period. Usually this is determined by when they are due. If you have a lot of bills due at once you will have to split them up so that some are paid early.

If you manage to pay all of your monthly obligations, feed yourself, keep your car running, and have money to set back in savings, you are doing a great job of budgeting for the month. If you find that you are a bit short at the end of the month, you are probably spending too much earlier in the month and will need to reevaluate your spending habits. This may mean budgeting by payday for a couple of months to get used to how to break up your spending and bills.

Chapter 10: Planning For The Future

"Do not save what is left after spending, but spend what is left after saving."

~ Warren Buffet

Many financial experts agree that one of the first steps to get yourself out of debt is to have an emergency fund. This fund acts like a buffer between you and your credit cards. If you have this money to use, you won't have to resort to credit cards and this will help keep you out of debt. $1000 is a good start for an emergency fund.

This is great, you may think, but if I'm in debt, how am I going to come up with another thousand dollars? There are two ways: spend less or make more. I suggest both. You can take any money you don't need to spend from your budget and start saving it. Depending on how much you are able to save per month, you may need to also earn more money. If you are paid hourly or on commission, you may have to work harder, or if you have a salary job, you may need to pick up a weekend job. You don't need to keep the job second job forever, or put in all those extra hours in your first job permanently, but financial peace of mind is worth a short term loss of free time.

Saving an extra thousand dollars may take quite a long time if your non-negotiable expenses are close to your income. Consider either a traditional part time job, or some other options listed below.

Sitting: Baby, house or pet. A reliable, mature babysitter makes $15 per hour in many areas of the country. 66 hours and 40 minutes of babysitting will give you a thousand dollars.

Collect all your loose change. I was shocked when I went through my house and collected all the change that was lying around. I had over $100 just sitting around. Places to look include: your bedside table, your desk or home office, under sofa and chair cushions, the laundry room, your car ashtray, the kitchen junk drawer, the bottoms of old purses, and any jars you tend to toss coins into because you don't want to carry them around.

Sell your things. You can have a yard sale or sell things on Craigslist. This is a particularly good idea for items you aren't using any more, like baby furniture, bicycles that are too small for your children, etc.

Dog walking. This is a great job for your non-working hours, particularly if you don't have a 9 to 5 job. You'll get a little exercise, some fresh air and money. What more could you want?

Bartending and wait staff. If you need money faster than the 2 weeks a "regular" part time job will pay, look for a job that people tip for, like bartender and wait staff. You can increase your tips by being friendly and helpful.

Work online. If you can write, edit or program, there are a lot of people looking to hire you for short term jobs. A few months of part time work and you'll have a your emergency fund filled.

Use your imagination. Your unique set of talents are valuable to people, all you need to do is figure out how to have people pay for them.

No matter which of these (or any other) options you choose, consider keeping the work until you have finished paying down all your debt. The process will go faster and rather than spending money, you'll be earning it.

It may not be easy to keep up with a second job and this is where your long term goal comes in to play. Spend some time every week thinking about your goal and how you will feel once you've achieved it.

Identification of long-term goals

Sure, life is much more fun with surprises. Sometimes, it is like hoping to win a lottery while spending your money on another fancy dress or home renovation. If you do not know where to go, how are you supposed to get there? Your long-term goals are going to help here. Long-term goals help you at every step of life. Discussing the life-goals with your significant other helps you identify the relationship with money. If you do not plan to live till tomorrow, there is no point of saving money. Sending your son to the college means you need to save a good sum! Owning a property means you were good in saving some bucks.

Here are some tips to establish long-term financial goals:

· What are my fantasy dreams? What hobbies do I want to pursue?

· How much value do I assign to the college education?

· What values do I want to hold in my life and the lives of my children?

· How soon do I plan to pay me outstanding debts?

· What things do I fear most?

Financial pressure is the worst nightmare for men and without a doubt 2.2 million Americans are suffering from this nightmare. Search the internet for quick money making schemes and you will find nothing, but junk content. Does that mean there is no way to make quick money? Sure, there are ways to earn thousands of dollars each day, but you cannot find them with a debt management mindset. At the end of this book, I am going to discuss proven money making ideas like the stock exchange market, and internet marketing. Quick money comes from planning. You can get a few bucks by selling old stuff, but we need a steady income source to live in peace. That peace only comes from having multiple income sources.

I have been in debt for over four years. It took almost 1.5 years to pay all the outstanding dues. Most people consider it a terrible time of your life. When I look back to ponder over my mistakes, I can relate that I have learned many valuable lessons of life. Financial crises teaches you something that the most valuable possessions cannot. The first test happens with your relationships. You just have to decide one thing. Either you can talk about money or you can save the relationship.

It is important to talk separately with each other about financial issues. At the end of life, people do not wish to spend more time in office. They wished they had spent more time with their children and spouse/soul mate. Being in debt is no fun. There will be many heartbreaking moments when your painful heart shares the sorrow with silent lips. I know these moments. It is painful to see your child suffering from fever and knowing that you only have 50$ in the pocket. You do not know where the next check is coming. The debt is increasing, and the credit card loan is creating problems. Breathe deeply and remind you of thousand others who are going through the same situation. Think about the time when you conquered the task. Nobody believed you, but you knew it was possible!

Think of the life happiest moment. You may note that the happiest moment has nothing to do with finance. You can be happy regardless of the amount of debt. We are going to play a game. It is a game that pays your debt. Here are some rules of this game:

· Firmly believe in yourself. Difficulties come not to break you, but to challenge you. Accept the challenge and win over it.

· Start a simple life. We do not need more. More increases complexities. Complex life structure is void of happiness & excitement. Aim for an excited life.

· Promise yourself to visit the wonderland of your dreams. Name 3 places that you would like to visit before you die. Plan to visit those places in next 3-5 years. Make it your goal. Promise to spend time in those three best places. Have faith in yourself and let me show you the path.

Start taking action. When you start something, you separate yourself from the rest of 90% population. Courage and little faith are required to do the job.

Chapter 11: Autopilot And Trim

Here we will discuss two strategies you can use to better spend your money, invest, and save. These will help you on your way towards your new life. They are focused on taking the hassle out of most of the things we do to keep our finances in tip-top shape.

AutoPiloting

As the name suggests, autopiloting means automating your savings and investments. This means that every time you get paid, a predetermined portion of your money is sent towards your savings accounts, bills, and investments (Weliver, 2019). Many companies and carriers offer this option, so instead of making payments yourself, the money could be withdrawn from your account on a set date.

This is good for several reasons. It means you do not have to do the mundane, sometimes stressful task of paying all your bills yourself. That gets taken care of for you and saves you a lot of time. The other benefit is the money that is left over in your account you are free to do with it as you see fit because you have already taken care of all your financial commitments. That is a freeing feeling.

Trim

While autopilot is a good strategy to use, it stops being beneficial when applied to services and subscriptions that are unnecessary, like premium cable. Subscriptions are things like Netflix, Hulu, YouTube Premium, gym memberships, and magazines. Many of these subscriptions can pile up and drain our money. This happens for two reasons. The first is that we forget the number of subscriptions we have made. It is challenging to keep track of all of them and cancel them. It can be overwhelming to go to each one of your subscriptions and cancel. Some providers make it easy; some make it difficult to do. As a precaution; you should be wary of free trials that say you can cancel at any time. The fact you can cancel at any time is great. But, companies that offer free trials bet on the fact that you will forget to cancel your subscription or be too lazy to do so, which happens often enough. It is a business tactic.

Trim is a free service that uses your credit card and bank information to show your long-forgotten subscriptions. Canceling your subscriptions on the service is easy. You just ask Trim to do it for you, and it will. The service also has a lot of other features. It can negotiate deals on your phone, internet, cable, and medical bills to find what is best for you. It really helps shed unnecessary costs. You will have more money in your pocket to spend, save, or invest.

Chapter 12: Make Your Budget Realistic

Now let's talk about being realistic. If you are living paycheck to paycheck right now, your first order of business is to get control of your money so you aren't living in this viscous cycle anymore. Once you've made your budget, you will be able to see exactly where your money is going. If you have high electric bills, you might think of turning the thermostat up or down a little bit to help lessen that cost. If your food bills are high, look for alternative markets to shop in, and/or check the supermarket flyers each week before you go shopping to know where the best deals are. If you can make one trip and not go out of your way to visit a couple of different markets, all you've invested is time.

Most supermarkets put their weekly ads online now, so you can check them at any time. And if you are really industrious, you can go to the various coupon sites, like couponsurfer.com, and search for coupons. The Sunday paper is also a great source for coupons for the things you usually buy. We would advise against clipping coupons for other items as you might be tempted to buy them and your grocery bill will go up.

Another good way to keep your grocery bill in check is to take just enough cash with you to pay for the items you've budgeted for. That way, you can't impulse buy. If you do, something vital may not get purchased.

So, once you've got a little extra breathing room, you start building your emergency fund. You also budget a little for yourselves for doing such a great job. It may only be enough for a quesadilla from Taco Bell, but that's one meal you don't have to cook, and, you get to get out of the house to eat it.

Next, you start paying off your debts, least first. As you do this, you create more money in the budget because you no longer have the payments for the debts you pay off. Use that money to continue paying off debt and to fill out your emergency fund. Soon, you will be debt free, have an emergency fund to turn to, if need be, and have some extra money in your budget every month.

Now, that extra money needs to go somewhere. Don't spend it! Start another fund: a college fund, retirement fund, vacation fund, or, if you're self-employed, a fund to pay your taxes at the end of the year. You can save for big purchases like TVs, furniture, and cars. Still leave a little for yourselves, just be prudent about it.

The same logic applies to those in the middle income ranges. In your case, though you likely are not living paycheck to paycheck, there is probably a lot that can be trimmed from your spending. You would be surprised how many people live beyond their means.

Start by making sure your income exceeds your expenses. If not, you need to make some major changes. Whether you are in this situation or not, you must sit down and take a serious look at your spending. One way to help you trim expenses is to look at what something costs you per month, or per year.

For instance, that cup of Starbuck's you buy every day on the way to work costs $3.85. If you work 5 days a week, that's $83.42 per month! Yearly, you are spending $1001.00 on Starbuck's. Don't you think you could do something more constructive with that money? Like maybe start an emergency fund? If you apply that logic to all of your "discretionary" expenses, those that you don't have to pay, you can decide whether the overall cost is worth it to you.

Once you've gotten a handle on your money and started your emergency fund, have a little fun. You deserve it. Then start paying down your debts. After you've accomplished this, or during the process, you will have more money in the budget from not having to make payments to your creditors anymore. Begin your college fund, or retirement fund, and/or vacation fund. Start funds for a new car, a new dining room suite, etc. Remember the old adage, pay yourself first. In other words, become prosperous through the use of this budget rather than blowing your extra money whenever you get it.

Even if you are in the higher income brackets, you still need a budget. You need to know what is coming in and what is going out just as much as anyone. And, you are just as prone to live outside your means. So, get a hold of your financial story with a budget. Then, set up an emergency fund appropriate for you. For instance, if you have three boys under 25 and they all drive Maserati's, then you will need a much larger emergency fund than most.

You will almost certainly have some debt. Pay it down next. When you have accomplished that, start your funds. You may already have a retirement plan, but many allow you to contribute also.

And don't forget, just because you have a comfortable income, doesn't mean you don't have waste in your budget. Clean it out using the tips and ideas we have already discussed and you may find that cruise to be closer than you think.

Chapter 13: It Is Time To Escape Your Debt

When you have a budget that is working for you, you will be able to pay off your debt with less stress. Debt is not easy to avoid. We all have some amount of debt we are hoping to pay off as quickly as possible and some of us are completely unaware of how certain debts are keeping us stuck in our money problems. Not all debt is bad. You need to show lenders that you are able to pay back money you borrow responsibly and the only way to prove this is if you have some kind of debt that you are actively paying back.

What we often neglect to understand is that certain debts will keep you stuck in financial strain indefinitely if you don't make the commitment to pay them off.

Types of Debt

There are a number of different types of debt we accumulate over our lifetime. We can most of the time not avoid having a small amount of debt attached to our name but many of us have a great deal of debt that is causing us to stay stuck in our money struggles. While some debt can be beneficial others are just damaging if not paid off in full as soon as you acquire them. These types of destructive debts are what keep us paying more than we have on things we could do without or at least waited to purchase.

Secured debt

Secured debts are those that allow you to borrow a certain amount of money under the stipulation that an asset is underlying if you are unable to pay back the loan. A car loan is the perfect example of this type of debt. You get approved for a certain amount of cash to pay for a new car, the purchased car is the lien. If you are unable to make the payments on the loan, then the car can be repossessed and sold to cover what you haven't paid. These loans are fairly straightforward and have low to moderate interest rates.

Unsecured debt

Unsecured loans are those that are offered in good faith alone. You do not need to put anything up for lien or as collateral to receive this type of loan. If you do fail to make the repayments the lender can sue you, which is never an ideal option as this is quite costly. Instead, lenders tend to add on a high-interest rate for unsecured loans. Medical bills, membership contracts for a gym or country club, and credit cards are some examples of unsecured debt that you can incur.

Revolving debt

Revolving debt refers to a set money limit that a borrower can use on a recurring basis. They can be in the form of a credit card or a line of credit. The borrower is expected to pay a minimal amount each month based on how much of the credit limit they have spent. Revolving debt can be a secured or unsecured debt so you can have a low or a high-interest rate.

Mortgages

Mortgages are long-term large sum loans. They are taken out to purchase a new home and are a type of secured debt where the purchase property is the collateral. These loans tend to have a relatively low-interest rate and tend to have a repayment plan that lasts from 15 to 30 years

The number one debt that will keep you from your financial goals is credit card debt. This is a revolving debt which allows you to spend money you don't have each month even without having to pay to make what you already owe. The problem is most credit cards are unsecured so they come with a fairly high-interest rate, meaning you will end up owing far more the longer you allow for this debt to sit around unpaid.

The Effects of Credit Card Debt

Most of us have grown up with the thinking that whatever money we don't have we can easily cover by using a credit card. This buy now pay later option, has caused many to accumulate thousands of dollars in debt. Credit cards have allowed millions to live beyond their means.

You may be making the minimum payments each month but often if your credit limit is high and you have maxed out that limit, your monthly payments are barely covering the interest rates, so your bill only goes down a few dollars each month. Not being able to pay off your balance at the end of the month results in you having to pay more than what you originally did for what you purchased. These interest rates can change at any time as well. You may sign up for a card that offers a low-interest rate but after a few months, this interest rate can significantly increase. If you have a balance left on your card this balance gets hit with that higher interest rate and you get further behind.

It is incredibly enticing to buy now and worry about paying later. The instant gratification you get from being able to buy when you don't have the money can ruin your credit and keep you stuck in financial strain. The less you are able to pay on your balance each month the more you will end up paying. Since your interest rates will then be added to your remaining balance, this then gets charged the interest rate. You end up paying interest on your interests. This is why it takes so many of us a much longer time to pay off our credit card debt and in the end, we end up spending much more than we intended. All because of the instant gratification of being able to buy now.

Credit cards are an attractive way to spend money you don't have. As long as you pay the minimum balance each month you can spend until you reach the limit. The problem is that most of us spend the maximum limit without having the minimum payment on hand. This causes us to incur more debt and penalty fees that dig us deeper into debt. As mentioned, the interest you get charged on your remaining balance carries over each month.

These cards aren't just enticing because they allow you to make purchases now and pay for it later, many stores and card companies have special offers or discounts that make us believe we are getting our money's worth. You might have signed up because a store or company gave you a huge discount on your first purchases or gave you a number of months where you didn't have to worry about paying interest on your balance. These seem like smart spending choices. You get your first purchase for less than you intended to pay and then you don't have to worry about paying interest while you are paying off your balance. What ends up happening is when we don't have to worry about the interest, we tend to neglect to pay off the balance before the end of the no-interest time frame. By the time we realize we need to pay off the remaining balance, without getting hit with a high-interest rate, we don't have a plan in place to pay off the debt.

Not all credit cards are the same either. Many store retail cards tack on a much higher interest rate, but these cards can be easier to get for someone with a lower credit score. These types of cards also add on reward incentives to get people to use their cards more often. Some of these retail cards may have their logo on them but they partner with a credit company that allows you to use this card anywhere, not only in the store. The Amazon card is a prime example of this.

Paying Off Debt

Begin by first creating a spreadsheet that allows you to see how much credit card debt you actually have. You want to list all the credits you have and what the remaining balance is on each of them . Also, write what the current interest rate is on each of the cards. Once you have a clear vision of what your credit card debt looks like, there are two ways you can approach getting yourself out of credit card debt.

Pay off the smaller debts

With this first approach to paying off your debt, you will rank them from the highest balance to the lowest. Building off this exercise, you can begin to pay off each smaller debt first. This is a simple three-step process.

Step one: Organize debt from smallest to largest amounts.

Step two: Pay the minimum on larger debts, pay more than the minimum on the smallest debt.

Step three: Once the smallest debt is paid off, put that money towards the next biggest debt.

Pay the highest interest rates

Sometimes, paying the smaller debts means your bigger debts are going to grow much larger depending on the interest rates. If you have a debt or multiple debts that have significantly higher interest rates it might be wiser to pay these off first. This can be hard as you need to pay more than what the interest rate adds on plus enough to bring the balance down.

Step one: Organize your debt according to their interest rates with the highest being at the top and the lowest rates at the bottom.

Step two: Calculate how much you need to pay on the highest interest rate in order to cover the interest and bring down the monthly balance.

Step three: Pay on the highest rate debt until paid off in full. Then move the money you were paying on the first debt to the net highest rate.

Neither of these debt pay-off approaches are ideal. What is even more beneficial is that you won't have to recalculate how much money you allocate to debt pay-off. You already start with a set amount that you will pay each month and you just continue with this amount, moving more of it to the next debt each time you pay-off one. This allows you to quickly eliminate debt from your budget. Once that first debt is paid off, the others go down substantially since you have additional money being dispersed to the next debt.

Another option that you can look into is consolidating your debt to one card that offers a low-interest rate. This is not always the most effective way to pay off debt, especially if you haven't gotten into a good flow with sticking to a budget. You may find yourself constantly moving your debt from one low-interest rate to another, never actually addressing the issue or taking action to pay it off. Consequently, this can make it more feasible for you to pay off your debt by only having to worry about paying one account instead of multiple ones.

Chapter 14: What Are The Types Of Budgets For Companies?

Four Main Types of Budgets/Budgeting Methods

There are four regular sorts of spending plans that organizations use: (1) steady, (2) action based, (3) offer, and (4) zero-based. These four planning techniques each have their own points of interest and difficulties, which will be examined in more detail in this guide.

1. Gradual planning

Gradual planning takes a year ago's genuine figures and adds or subtracts a rate to acquire the present year's spending limit. It is the most widely recognized strategy for planning since it is straightforward and straightforward. Gradual planning is suitable to utilize if the essential cost drivers don't change from year to year. Be that as it may, there are a few issues with utilizing the strategy:

It is probably going to propagate wasteful aspects. For instance, if a chief realizes that there is a chance to develop his spending limit by 10% consistently, he will basically accept that open door to accomplish a greater spending plan, while not placing exertion into looking for approaches to reduce expenses or conserve.

It is probably going to bring about budgetary leeway. For instance, a chief may exaggerate the size of the spending that the group very so apparently the group is constantly under spending plan.

It is likewise prone to disregard outside drivers of action and execution. For instance, there is high swelling in certain information costs. Steady planning disregards any outer variables and essentially expect the cost will develop by, for instance, 10% this year.

2. Action based planning

Action based planning is a top-down planning approach that decides the measure of data sources required to help the objectives or yields set by the organization. For instance, an organization sets a yield focus of $100 million in incomes. The organization should initially decide the exercises that should be embraced to meet the business target, and afterward discover the expenses of doing these exercises.

3. Offer planning

In offer planning, the budgeter thinks about the accompanying inquiries:

For what reason is this sum remembered for the spending limit?

Does the thing make an incentive for clients, staff, or different partners?

Does the estimation of the thing exceed its expense? In the event that not, at that point is there another motivation behind why the expense is supported?

Incentive planning is actually an outlook about ensuring that everything that is remembered for the spending conveys an incentive for the business. Incentive planning means to dodge superfluous uses – despite the fact that it isn't as correctly focused on that objective as our last planning choice, zero-based planning.

4. Zero-based planning

As one of the most normally utilized planning strategies, zero-based planning begins with the suspicion that all division spending plans are zero and should be modified without any preparation. Chiefs must have the option to legitimize each and every cost. No consumptions are consequently "approved". Zero-based planning is tight, meaning to maintain a strategic distance from any consumptions that are not viewed as significant to the organization's effective (gainful) activity. This sort of base up planning can be a profoundly viable approach to "shake things up".

The zero-based methodology is great to utilize when there is a pressing requirement for cost regulation, for instance, in a circumstance where an organization is experiencing a money related rebuilding or a significant financial or advertise downturn that expects it to decrease the spending limit drastically.

Zero-based planning is most appropriate for tending to optional expenses as opposed to fundamental working expenses. Be that as it may, it tends to be an amazingly tedious methodology, such a large number of organizations just utilize this methodology every so often.

Levels of Involvement in Budgeting Process

We need purchase in and acknowledgment from the whole association in the planning procedure, yet we likewise need a well-characterized spending plan and one that isn't controlled by individuals. There is constantly an exchange off between objective coinciding and inclusion. The three topics laid out beneath should be thought about with a wide range of spending plans.

Forced planning

Forced planning is a top-down procedure where officials cling to an objective that they set for the organization. Administrators pursue the objectives and force spending focuses for exercises and expenses. It tends to be compelling if an organization is in a turnaround circumstance where they have to meet some troublesome objectives, yet there may be next to no objective compatibility.

Arranged planning

Arranged planning is a blend of both top-down and base up planning techniques. Officials may layout a portion of the objectives they might want to hit, and yet, there is shared obligation regarding spending arrangement among chiefs and representatives. This expanded contribution in the planning procedure by lower-level representatives may make it simpler to hold fast to spending focuses, as the workers feel like they have an increasingly close to home enthusiasm for the achievement of the spending plan.

Participative planning

Participative planning is a move up approach where representatives work from the base up to prescribe focuses to the officials. The administrators may give some info, however they pretty much accept the suggestions as given by office chiefs and different representatives (sensibly speaking, obviously). Activities are treated as self-ruling auxiliaries and are given a ton of opportunity to set up the financial limit.

5 Types of Budgets for Businesses

There are a wide range of kinds of spending plans. Would you be able to name 5?

Spending plans assist organizations with following and deal with their assets.

Organizations utilize an assortment of spending plans to gauge their spending and create viable methodologies for amplifying their advantages and incomes. The accompanying sorts of spending plans are normally utilized by organizations:

Ace Budget

An ace spending plan is a total of an organization's individual spending plans intended to exhibit a total image of its money related action and wellbeing. The ace spending joins factors like deals, working costs, resources, and salary streams to enable organizations to build up objectives and assess their general execution, just as that of individual cost focuses inside the association. Ace spending plans are regularly utilized in bigger organizations to keep every single individual administrator adjusted.

Working Budget

A working spending plan is an estimate and examination of anticipated pay and costs through the span of a predefined timeframe. To make an exact picture, working spending plans must record for elements, for example, deals, creation, work costs, materials costs, overhead, fabricating costs, and authoritative costs. Working spending plans are by and large made on a week by week, month to month, or yearly premise. A director may contrast these reports a seemingly endless amount of time after month with check whether an organization is overspending on provisions.

Income Budget

An income spending plan is a methods for anticipating how and when money comes in and streams out of a business inside a predetermined timeframe. It tends to be valuable in helping an organization decide if it's dealing with its money admirably. Income spending plans consider factors, for example, creditor liabilities and records receivable to survey whether an organization has plentiful money close by to keep working, the degree to which it is utilizing its money beneficially, and its probability of producing money sooner rather than later. A development organization, for instance, may utilize its income spending plan to decide if it can begin another structure venture before getting paid for the work it has in progress.

Money related Budget

A money related spending presents an organization's methodology for dealing with its advantages, income, pay, and costs. A budgetary spending plan is utilized to set up an image of an organization's money related wellbeing and present a far reaching review of its spending comparative with incomes from center tasks. A product organization, for example, may utilize its monetary spending plan to decide its incentive with regards to an open stock offering or merger.

Static Budget

A static spending plan is a fixed spending that remaining parts unaltered paying little heed to changes in elements, for example, deals volume or income. A pipes supply organization, for instance, may have a static spending plan set up every year for warehousing and capacity, paying little respect to how a lot of stock it moves in and out because of expanded or diminished deals.

10 Types of Budget that exist for Businesses

Spending limit is characterized as an arrangement, budgetary in nature, for a predefined period as a rule for a time of one year. For instance, a whole of cash apportioned for a time of one year. It is a necessary piece of nearly everything be it government, associations, private ventures, or even a family unit.

The spending makes its quality all over the place and guarantees legitimate adherence to it since the intersection of the financial backing is certainly not a decent sign yet the underutilizing spending plan is the point. Overspending of the spending shows an absence of arranging and overseeing expenses and pay. A perfect spending plan should cover every one of the costs and leave somewhat surplus for extra and unanticipated costs.

Following are 10 unique sorts of Budget. These are ordinarily utilized in pretty much every association except different organizations may require various spending plans relying upon their temperament of the business and their particular necessities.

Here are the 10 Types of Budgets that Businesses can utilize

1) Cash stream spending plan

Foreseeing when and how the money will stream in or out of the business is known as an income spending plan. The income spending plan is typically determined for a particular time, for instance, a year. Income spending plan is valuable for the association to deal with its money and it additionally considers factors, for example, records of sales creditor liabilities to decide if an organization has adequate income in hands for proceeding with its activities.

Income is likewise significant in deciding significant speculation choices of the organization. A Pharmaceutical organization, for instance, may utilize its income spending plan to foresee whether it can begin putting resources into another item or not. Numerous associations contribute the extra income produced in the wake of dealing with all costs into social and magnanimous work which falls under corporate social duty.

Sorts of Budget - 1

2) Operating Budget

A conjecture of anticipated pay and costs alongside its investigation through the span of a particular timeframe is known as the working spending plan. Working spending plan must incorporate factors, for example, creation, work cost, and so forth to give a reasonable picture to the organization.

The particular timespan for working spending plan is week after week, month to month, quarterly, half yearly or yearly relying upon the comfort of the association. An ordinary month on month or quarter on quarter investigation of these reports helps in the assurance of overspending of spending plans.

3) Financial spending plan

The organization methodology for overseeing it resources pay and costs and other monetary perspectives are available in the money related spending plan. The budgetary spending paints the general image of the monetary soundness of the organization and a review of it going through as per its incomes from center tasks.

A money related spending plan is a solid determinant of steadiness of the organization and a positive budgetary spending implies great business and sound association why the negative monetary spending plan demonstrates plausible issues.

4) Sales Budget

This sort of spending gives some normal deals income and costs and selling for the association for a particular timeframe. It is the foundation of the association or it is otherwise called the operational hub since it is the inception on which are stores are additionally based. Deals gauging assumes a significant job and assurance of offers spending plan is both ought to be appropriate for further things to fall set up.

Anticipating of offers should be possible either in amount or worth relying upon the association. In the event of overwhelming equipment's, it very well may be referenced in amount astute if there should be an occurrence of FMCG items business worth might be referenced. Legitimate gauging is fundamental for deals spending plan since a conjecture misses the business spending plan may go of which would imply that the activities and accessibility of materials would be influenced.

5) Production spending plan

Deals spending structures the reason for the arrangement of the generation spending plan. Stock levels are likewise thought about alongside the assembling system of the association. The creation spending plan is valuable in deciding the expense of generation which thusly will choose the cost of the item. Each association has an alternate kind of generation spending plan.

For the most part, the financial backing is separated into creation per article every month and the probable interest produced from the market. In the event that the Sales and request go sequential it would be the obligation of the association to alter their generation spending plans in like manner.

6) Overheads Budget

Overheads Budget is the sort of Budget which includes every one of the expenses and costs required for a predefined timeframe of creation. This incorporates however isn't constrained to aberrant work, immediate and roundabout processing plant costs, and other related costs.

An assortment of the considerable number of overheads of the manufacturing plant, administrator, circulation and so on is incorporated under Overheads Budget. For the most part, the monetary allowance is readied office astute for proficient command over the expenses. The assembling costs are additionally partitioned into Fixed, semi-variable and variable expenses.

7) Personnel Budget

Faculty Budget is one of the pivotal kinds of the spending which covers the labor spending plan for the particular time frame. Work hours, laborers grade, costs and so forth. Since it deals with all the staff, and productive working of an association relies upon the installment of the representatives, this is one of the significant kinds of spending plan.

8) Marketing Budget

The financial backing allotted to the Marketing division is known as the Marketing Budget. This sort of Budget deals with all the showcasing and limited time exercises of the organization for the clients. A definitive point of promoting is to help the business group to create more business.

The promoting spending plan for the year chooses the quantity of exercises to be done in one budgetary year. The exercises include a blend of occasions, advancements, and publicizing so as to elevate the item to the client.

9) Static Budget

Static Budget is like Fixed expenses. These are the costs which are static and stay unaltered over an extensive stretch of time and it could be plumbing supply costs, stockroom cost, production line support and so forth. It isn't affected by the business volume or some other changes in the association.

10) Master Budget

A mix of all the individual spending plans of the organization, which gives a total image of the general monetary image of the association is called as Master Budget. All the departmental spending plans like Sales, Marketing, Overheads and so forth spending plans are consolidated to get ready Master Budget. Setting up connection in every one of the offices is basic and ace spending deals with that. The bigger the association, the helpful is ace spending plan since gives one view over every one of the offices.

Chapter 15: Put Your Mind At Ease About The Future

Unexpected expenses can be caused by different things. You may have emergency home repairs or additional power and heat usage. You may also have unexpected car repair bills, insurance premiums, emergency hospitalization, additional school fees, medications, higher gym membership rates, etc. These costs are unexpected. Nevertheless, you should still be prepared, whether or not you know they are coming.

How to Budget and Save for Unexpected Expenses?

Begin by listing down possible unexpected expenses, such as property taxes, home insurance, car insurance, car repairs, dental bills, eye checkups, winterization, and gifts for the holidays and other special occasions.

Check out last year's calendar, and your previous credit card and bank statements.

Find out what irregular expenses you used your credit card to pay for. If you have children, see to it that you take their tuition and school fees, music lessons, school bus, and sports commitments into consideration.

Tally the amounts to find out which ones are above and over your regular monthly expenses. Divide that by the number of paychecks you receive per year. For instance, if your periodic and irregular expenses totaled to $2,500 for the entire year, divide that by 26 if you get paid on a bi-weekly basis. You will get an amount close to $96. This means that you have to set aside $96 in another account so you can have money in case you need it. If you find it hard to set aside $100 per month, start with a smaller amount. For instance, you can start with $25. That should not be too hard on your pocket! Gradually, increase it until you arrived at your desired amount.

Set up a money management system to help you organize your finances. Electronic fund transfers are actually easier and much more convenient than traditional means since you no longer have to go to the bank or payment center. You can pay your bills via the Internet, anytime and anywhere. This can also help you save money on gas or fare.

Chapter 16: How To Travel On A Budget

Travelling has always been associated with quite a high cost. However, in the past few years, we've seen stories about people around the world who travel on limited budgets and just sheer will power – such as the couple who travelled from Bulgaria to India by hitch hiking! Of course, you might not want to do that as a full time occupation, but it is quite easy to travel on a budget.

There are several useful blogs and sites on the internet that offer information on how to travel on a budget, what places are the best to stay, what sights are worth seeing, so on and so forth; all offering pictorial evidence to prove their point! All of which can be done from the comfort of your chair at home.

In this section, we will look at how you can get the maximum out of your budget holiday!

1. Find out about deals on air, coach, rail or ship or ferry deals on the internet. There are several providers who offer a fantastic way to do this. Ensure that you take the most advantage of budget carriers – air, rail and coach. These providers usually have a much cheaper rate for common destinations as mainstream carriers for a price that is either half or even less than that.

You can use Amtrak for travel by rail in the U.S., for Europe, you can think about Eurail for non-EU individuals, or Interrail for EU citizens. Both offer international passes for rail travel.

You can use coaches to travel inter city once you reach your destination. Greyhound in the U.S and Eurolines in Europe offer deals on coach tickets. Some travel routes are cross country, so check out what best can be offered. Megabus is another European provider who offers travel among nearly 45 European countries, apart from travel routes in the North American continent.

Use websites such as sky scanner, or kayak or even travel supermarket to find out cheap ways to fly. These websites offer comparison data on flight tickets and also help you find the cheapest ticket. Mediator hosting sites such as Travelocity and Opodo also offer discount deals and trips for flights.

If you wish to travel by ship or cruise, this can be a cheap deal if you get accommodation and meals included in the price. There are operators such as Star cruises and Cunard who operate on the transatlantic route. You also have websites such as The Cruise People which compare cruise prices for you.

Hack: Remember to clear your cookies every time you search for tickets or fares. Browsers remember these little bits of information, and websites use them to bump the prices up every time you revisit them while searching for options and more options. Once you've made your mind up about the ticket, clear your browser history, delete the cookies, and then boot up the website. You'd be surprised at the price difference!

2. When it comes to accommodation, the internet is your friend. Search online for information and get a list of all the backpacker hostels and youth hostels you can find in the place you want to go to. Don't forget, you just need a place to sleep. Doesn't necessarily mean it has to be first class.

You can additionally consider travelling by sleeper trains to cover the distance between journey points, and get a good bit of sleep in too!

Hack: The YMCA is usually present in almost every city. Hostels such as these have a much cheaper option to stay. Remember, when you go on a holiday, you will spend the majority of the day travelling. It doesn't make much sense to spend a fortune on a hotel room that you will barely use for a few hours, that too, to get a few hours of kip in.

3. If you have friends in the place you want to visit, check with them if you can stay with them to save on living expenses. Remember to follow the three day rule, so you want to make sure you don't overstay your welcome.

Be a good guest, and keep your area clean and tidy, make the bed when you wake up, and help out with the chores.

Hack: Use websites such as Travelsherpa and others, that have local residents host travellers. The world is opening up, and you get to live with local residents. Remember the 3 day rule, and of course, don't forget to rate your host. Share the love!

4. Save money by walking around. A Lot! Visit cheap attractions or free attractions, and use cheap public transportation or

shuttle busses. You learn a lot more about a place by travelling on foot, with the bonus of saving money on transportation.

Talk to locals and tourists who appear friendly, this is your biggest resource when it comes to finding out more information on what to see and what to avoid. Talk to travel guides on how to stay for longer without spending a lot.

Make sure you check for information online before you visit a place so that you can get a deal for cheap.

Hack: Most centres of entertainment, or attractions offer discounts for pre-booking. As soon as you have decided to visit a place, google the attractions and look for cheap deals for advance booking. Saves you the hassle of waiting in line, and is a lot cheaper than booking tickets on the same day, or even in the week of your intended visit.

5. One of the things to remember when travelling about is to bring your own food.

Bring along soup packets and noodles so that you can travel for a long time with a small amount of money. Remember that you are there for the adventure, and not to experience first class dining. If not with soup packets, find local food places where you can eat for a lot less with the added bonus of experiencing the local culture and getting a whole lot more tasty food.

Take a lot of pictures, make new memories, create a travel log that will bring a smile on your face every time you open it!

Hack: Carry sachets of coffee and creamer, a few biscuit packets. Most accommodations have a kettle and have clean drinking water. Doesn't take much effort or cost to have a nice brew! The kettle serves its purpose in making the instant noodles too!

6. When booking your accommodation online, book it only for the first night. In this way, you'll have a place to crash when you land, and you don't have to worry

about finding another place. You can then walk about the next day and find places that are more suitable to your budget. You can also leave your luggage at this place without having to cart it around while looking for the new place.

There are of course a whole lot of other tips and tricks that you can do when you're travelling to make sure that you get the best out of the experience, and not just the place. All you need to do, is read some more!

Hack: Check websites such as AirBnB and Agoda, apart from TripAdvisor and others, all of which offer the best price. As with the travel tickets, remember to clear your cookies in the browser, restart the website and make your booking. It may take a few more minutes, but it will be worth it when you have an additional $100 - $200 for spending cash!

Maximize Your Dollar

In this section, we will see how to stretch your dollar. From investments, to buying smart, looking for deals, and getting the best value for everything you purchase, there is always a cheaper alternative.

There are several things that you can do to extend your dollar – from non-branded light bulbs instead of branded LED's(the components inside are all the same), to a regular toothbrush instead of the fancy electric one that can navigate you to the moon, to saving in recurring deposit accounts in the bank that offer you a high rate of investment, apart from smart stock market buying and selling; try to get the maximum value for every dollar that you spend.

It's quite easy to forget that at the end of it all, money is a tool that should be used to make your life comfortable, not the other way around where you slog all day and night, just to make enough to get by.

1. Hire a financial planner. Or at least get a few sessions in with someone who does it

for a living. They know how to maximize each dollar's value, and how to minimize expenses and increase savings.

2. Budget your expenses. Once you've put aside money, know what it is that you use regularly. Non-perishable consumables like dishwash, soaps, household commodities have prolonged shelf lives. Places like Costco and Walmart offer sales on bulk purchases where you can save a lot of money on the cost per item. Simply buy in bulk and store, use the commodities over the year.

3. With food items, buy meats and vegetables that can be frozen. As with the non-perishables, buy these in bulk and store them in the freezer, using them as required. This often works out cheaper than having to buy smaller portions on a daily basis for meals. All it requires is a bit of effective time management and planning, and you'll not just have quite a bit to eat, but you'd also be able to experiment and cook whatever you'd fancy, right at home!

4. If you are a small business owner, or have a hobby business, try and always account your purchases before accounting for your taxes. Pre tax expenses are usually exempt from tax if you have a business. You'd end up paying the tax only on the amount left over after all your expenses are done. As always, check with your financial planner or accountant.

5. Try to get coupons and flyers on sales. Visit websites including Groupon to usually get anywhere between a 10% − 90% discount on products, items, holidays, and a whole host of other things. Discount websites offer the same product that you want, at a much cheaper price. The most you'd have to put up with is a bit of comparative research and a bit of patience while the product is delivered to you.

6. The power of the Internet. Use it to the maximum. We live in a world that is constantly in connection with everything else in and on it. Use the internet to find out ways and means you can save, from maxing out your 401K, to investing in

stocks and bonds, to finding discounts on great deals (Black Friday and Boxing day Sales included); compare results to make sure that you do not end up spending more than required.

7. Read the fine print always. Remember that there are more often than not, hidden costs and charges that you can incur. Always check when purchasing something, what the full price that you pay will be. In case of credit cards and loans, check on penalties and interest rates. Know how many days of interest free billing you have before you start getting charged anywhere between 15 to 30% interest on that shirt you bought from the GAP. Pay it off so that you don't spend as much.

8. Live pre-paid. Pay as you go options are actually fantastic as they let you know how much you get for your dollar. From the talk time on your phone, to how much gas and electricity you have left to use. The options to top up are quite easily accessible, and you always know how much you are spending. Pre-paid spending

also means that you do not have to worry about additional expenses unless it is an emergency – no hidden or unexpected costs later.

9. Learn to negotiate. The art of haggling is something that I was quite embarrassed about, but when I saw how much savings I made, it made so much more sense. Read up about the average pricing of what it is that you are going to buy – the new phone on the market, a tooth repair procedure, medical tests, a second hand car, whatever. If you know the price of the product, chances are a fair bit of haggling can get you a much cheaper price if you negotiate with the sales person. This can be anyone, from the local grocer at the farmers market, to the dentist.

In case of medical expenses, remember to find out from your insurer how much a procedure will cost approximately and then call the local doctor or test center and for a fair bit of haggling, you can get up to about 50% off on your bill. Same procedure, half the price. Simples.

10. Plan your expenses. Always keep some money stashed aside for a rainy day (or a sunny day, if you fancy a break or a holiday). Don't let anything take you by surprise. In any and all eventualities, a sensible financial plan will always keep you secure. Just takes a bit of prior planning. Having said that, teach yourself to rigorously stick to the plan once you've made it. After all, it is YOUR MONEY that you want to save.

Chapter 17: Simple Tips That Will Make Your Budget Work For You

Keep Track of your Expenses

By your expenses, I mean all of them even your small ones as discussed above. Some of the major expenses like your rent are easy because you can remember them. It is easy though to lose track of the small expenses. To help you keep track of them you can ensure that you keep the receipts for recording or do the recording after the day's purchases. Another way is to include them under the miscellaneous items. This will give you a clear picture of what is going on with your finances. You can use the envelop system to make this easier for you. But if you prefer paying electronically, you can be depositing all the money that you need to spend for every expenditure item in an operating bank account or debit card. You can then be making payment from that card only. It is easy to check the statements to know whatever it is you purchased when and where.

Update your budget daily

This is just to help you not forget especially the tiny little purchases. You can use Evernote to record your expenses whenever you incur them. This will ensure there's no big time difference between when you incurred the expenditure and when you record it. Make the most of cloud storage services like Dropbox to make it easy to update your document whenever and wherever you want.

Use Accurate Description

Instead of stating the store that you shopped, you are better off stating the specific things that you bought from the store. You can summarize this by putting them into categories like; clothing, groceries or household cleaning supplies.

Budget by the month and not by the paycheck

We all earn at different times, so instead of budgeting by the time that your paycheck sets in, you are better off budgeting on a monthly basis. This provides a long enough period and the chance of being able to start afresh with every new month. It also helps in that if you have a bad month, it will be over and be in the past.

Plan for Occasional Expenses

It is good to put aside some money for different occasions that may occur throughout the year especially if you are working on a very strict budget. You can decide to group these things under the miscellaneous. Irregular pay may also make the budget a little difficult to work with. However, it is still feasible; you can try to estimate the minimum that you earn and center your budget on it. In this case, if you get any extras, you can put it aside for the bad days.

You May Encounter Problems With Your Budget If:

It is too complicated than it needs to be

It does not reflect your values; this happens especially if you decide to copy another person's working budget

It does not reflect the reality; it should be based on your real income and your expenses must correspond to the ones that you have in reality and not those you think you incurred.

It seems like a chore; make budgeting fun because that is what its purpose in your life should be. To make you enjoy life!

It is not realistic; remember we talked about following the SMART acronym when setting your goals and budget? Revisit that and things will be easier.

Be flexible

Do not feel limited to sticking to your budget. You may want to spend more on a particular month because you have some visitors; allow yourself to. Just make sure that you cut off some money from another expense that you can forgo to compensate on it.

Have some fun

Make sure that there is room in your budget to have some fun. This depends on how tight your budget is. However, you don't have to spend too much on yourself; let your budget have some allocation for the things that you can do to reward yourself. This is the only incentive that there can be to enable you to work harder. If your budget does not allow for this, then at times it becomes difficult to adhere to it.

Spend below your income

Do not spend more than you earn. You are well aware that there will always be holidays every year. Instead of waiting until that time to do your spending on major purchases, you can be buying the gifts throughout the year.

Avoid unnecessary debts

If something is not a long-term investment, then there is no need of going into debt because of it. Be able to identify these investments like a house or education. When buying something like a car, you should be aware that its value depreciates every year. It is not something that you want to go into debt for.

Chapter 18: Dealing With Major Events

There are a few things in life that come around rarely, whether it's once every few years or once in a lifetime. Budgeting and basic investing are designed to get you through normal times, but sometimes extraordinary things occur, and unless you have some idea of how to handle them properly, they can create huge setbacks in your financial planning.

Some of these are events are positive (like getting a better job). Others are good things but costly (a wedding), while others are entirely bad (medical expenses). It's important to make the most out of the good events, find a way to enjoy those that are positive but potentially costly without breaking the bank, and get through the bad ones without having your whole financial life thrown into chaos. Let's start with one of the best ones:

Getting a new job or a raise

Congrats! Depending on how your new job (or salary) compares to your old one, this can be anywhere from good to life changing. Unfortunately, a lot of people get caught up in celebrating and fail to take advantage of the positive position they're in.

The most important thing when it comes to getting a new job is that you negotiate your salary. Consider this – if you get a job offer of $50,000 and you negotiate it up to $55,000, you haven't just made an extra $5000. Because each time you get a raise, your new salary will be based on your old one, that extra $5000 will carry on through your entire working career. Next time you get a raise, instead of moving from $50,000 to $55,000, you'll be moving from $55,000 to $60,000 and so on. If you work for 35 more years, that's $175,000 of cash. If you invest that extra $5000 at 5% each year, then by the time you retire you'll have an extra $463,000. That's real money!

Thus, negotiating your salary is one of the easiest ways to have an enormous impact on your financial future. If you include the time it takes to do research on market salaries for your new position, you may spend four or five hours getting your salary increased – when else in your life will you be able to spend that little time and make hundreds of thousands of dollars over your lifetime as a result? Always, always, always negotiate.

These types of negotiations can be nerve-wracking, especially if you don't have a lot of experience. There are countless books on the topic that are worth reading (I highly recommend Getting More by Stuart Diamond), so I won't go into enormous detail, but there are a few things you should know:

For most salaried positions, it is expected that you'll negotiate. When they offer you $50,000, they probably have a budget of $55,000 or $60,000 for someone in your position. They purposefully leave themselves room to come up because they assume you will ask them to. It's not pushy or rude to ask for more money – it will seem stranger to a recruiter if you don't ask for more. Unless you request something completely outlandish, like double the initial offer, the worst thing they'll say is no.

Increases in salary are infinitely better than signing bonuses (well, not technically infinitely, but close). Sometimes if you request a $5000 increase in salary, you'll get offered a $5000 signing bonus instead. Stick to your guns and insist that it be in the salary, so that you get all the long term benefits I mentioned above. To compare to my earlier example, a $5000 signing bonus invested at 5% would get you about $28,000 by retirement, compared to the $463,000 from the $5000 salary increase.

When you're moving jobs, remember that your new salary should be about your new job, not your old one. Most employers will ask about your current salary during the interview process, and there's endless advice on how to deal with it that ranges from being honest to lying to refusing to answer. Again, I'll defer to the negotiation books on this one, but the one thing I'll say is to do your salary research on sites like Glassdoor and Comparably. Assuming you're interviewing with a larger company, you can probably find a pretty good idea of what your position pays. If it's substantially higher than what your old position paid, good – just make sure you keep that in mind while negotiating. If your old position paid $50,000 but everyone in your new position is getting $75,000, hold out for the $75,000 even if it sounds like a huge jump to you.

Whenever you're interviewing, try to interview at as many places as possible. Getting multiple job offers is absolutely the best thing you can do when it comes to salary negotiation. If you're interviewing at multiple employers and get an offer from one for your dream job, don't stop the interview process at the others – continue to work as hard as you can to get offers there, so you can use those to get paid even more at your dream job. Multiple offers give you leverage, which is the most valuable thing you can have in a negotiation.

If you do have multiple job offers that are all interesting, make sure you do a full comparison of their compensation. Don't just look at the salaries - benefits like a 401k, shorter commute, free food in the office and better insurance should be weighed. If you're getting other compensation like stock options, make sure you value them conservatively, since a bad stock market may make them worth less over time.

Once you've taken the new job or received a raise at your current one, it's important that you avoid lifestyle creep – letting yourself spend all of the extra money you're earning (or worse, spending even more than the extra). Be very conscious about how your extra income fits into your budget. If you want to use some of it for dining or other non-mandatory expenses, that's fine, but you should figure out how much of the increase you want to spend each month, adjust your budget accordingly and then stick to it.

One of the best ways to avoid lifestyle creep is to increase how much you're contributing to your 401k each time you get a raise. Increase your contribution amount, and you'll automatically save more each month and avoid being tempted by a bigger paycheck that you want to go out and spend.

Planned large one-time expenses

One of the reasons to save money and develop a solid financial plan is so that when you need to spend money, you can do so without worrying about how to come up with funds. Big events like weddings can be the highlights of your life, and they're even better when you aren't stressing about money.

When you have one of these events on the horizon, take a minute to assess where you stand financially. The biggest question here is how much you have saved up — whatever you do, don't spend more than you have. Some people simply must have an enormous, high-end wedding regardless of the cost, and when they can't afford it, they take out a loan. Please, please don't ever take out a loan to pay for an expense like this. Spending money that you already have sets you back a bit by reducing your savings, but that's okay — that's part of what savings are for. Taking out a loan, on the other hand, doesn't just reduce the amount of money that you have, it also reduces your ability to save by adding another expense that you have to pay every month. Even if you do have savings, try not to burn through all of them just because they're there. Figure out a reasonable budget for the event and stick to it, so you have a great time and money left over in the bank.

Every culture has its own traditions with weddings and other major events, so I certainly won't tell you exactly what to do. Still, try to remember that even if you want a big, extravagant event, the most important thing is the people that are there, and I promise you that they'll be glad to attend even if you decide only to have beer and wine at your wedding instead of a full open bar.

One last note, particularly about weddings – negotiate prices. Florists, event spaces, bartenders and other related services charge a huge premium as soon as they hear the word "wedding." If you don't believe me, call up a florist and ask them how much it will cost to have basic flowers for a wedding with 100 people. Have your spouse call later and ask how much it will cost to have basic flowers for a dinner with 100 people. I can almost guarantee the wedding flowers will be twice the price, if not more. That means there's lots of room left for the florist to come down in price and still make money, so get a few quotes and play them off against each other to get a reasonable rate.

Unplanned large one-time expenses

Large, unplanned expenses can be devastating not only because of their financial cost, but also because they're almost universally bad things – car accidents, medical bills, funerals and the like. This is a great reason to get your finances in place ahead of time. If you suffer a serious injury, financial security means the only thing you have to worry about is getting better.

When something does come up, take time to understand the costs you're going to incur. If it's a medical bill, spend time with the billing department at the hospital as well as your insurance company to find out exactly what insurance will cover and how much will be left to you. Take a similar approach for anything else unexpected – make sure that you understand the situation and your costs well.

Once you've done that, see how your costs stack up in comparison to your finances. Hopefully you'll have enough in your emergency fund to cover everything. If so, it may feel disappointing to have to hand over that much money, but take some time to appreciate that because of your planning, you were able to weather a crisis without any major impact on your day to day life.

If you can't cover everything with the cash you have available, try to work out a payment plan. This is frequently possible with hospitals – they recognize their bills can be large and tough to pay, so they'd rather work with you to figure out a way to get paid than just have you give up and pay them nothing. If you can pay over time without any additional interest or fees being tacked on, take advantage of that, as it's basically the equivalent of receiving a free loan.

On the other hand, if you need to pay more than you have available in your emergency fund, take stock of what other resources you have. If you've been saving money and investing it in the stock market, you can sell some of those investments to generate the cash you need. If you really have nothing available, look at possible loans. The company to which you owe money may be willing to let you pay over time with interest – if so, compare this to other possible options like taking a personal loan. Figure out what the cheapest way to get the money is, then make sure you pay off the debt and replenish your emergency fund as quickly as possible. Whatever you do, try to avoid just charging the bill to a credit card that you won't be able to pay off immediately – this is the most costly type of loan you can take out.

A couple of notes about some specific events that may come up and how to handle them:

Funerals – Funeral homes are frequently staffed by people who can only be described as vultures. They know that you're in a lot of pain and will use that to guilt you into spending more money than you should. They'll invoke the deceased and remind you that he or she really deserves the finest casket and service.

Don't let them play this game with you —
try to buy as little as possible directly from
them (Costco sells caskets at very
reasonable prices and can deliver them to
a funeral home for use). If you're really
feeling overwhelmed, ask a trusted friend
or associated who is not as close to the
deceased to help you when it comes to the
financial negotiations. An outside
perspective can really help to avoid
making mistakes that you might
otherwise.

Medical bills — As I mentioned above,
hospitals know that their bills are large
and can be tough to pay, so they're very
motivated to work with you. In addition to
offering payment plans, many of them will
also negotiate your bill down, especially if
you don't have insurance. Call their billing
department and ask what the price is if
you settle your bill immediately in cash.
Once they give you a price, tell them you
don't think you can afford it and try to
haggle it down further.

Major lifestyle changes

If you're single and you live by yourself, it's relatively easy to make a financial plan. You only have to worry about one person, and you have a perfect understanding of that person's needs, wants and desires. If that's you right now, great – the best time to start planning is when things are simple, and you have some time to start building up a nest egg before a future in which other people may count on your and your money.

It's likely, though, that your life won't stay so simple. You'll see some big changes that will make things more complex (but will also make your life better and more fulfilling), like getting married and having children. When those happen, you'll need to make sure to adjust your financial plan accordingly.

First, let's talk about marriage. It's clichéd but true advice that one of the most fundamental pieces of a successful relationship is communication, and that's absolutely the case when it comes to money. If you're lucky, you'll be marrying someone who also understands the value of a financial plan and has been working to save and invest. In that case, you'll just need to merge your plans together – first, do the basics of determining your collective income and expenses to get a grasp on your new financial life. After that, talk about the big picture: what kind of lifestyle do you want, do you want to have children, where do you want to live and all of the other major decisions and compromises that come with sharing your life with someone else. Using the tools in this book, make sure that your saving and investing is going to put you on the road to a happy life that fulfills all of your dreams!

Unfortunately, because it's somewhat taboo to talk about finances in our society, many couples get quite far into their relationships without having a serious discussion about money. Given this, it's fully possible that you'll find at some point either before or after your wedding that you have very different ideas about personal finance. If you end up in this situation, have a serious discussion about your differences. Some of them may relate to lifestyle – you're happy retiring to a cabin in the woods, while your spouse or spouse-to-be has always pictured life in a Manhattan penthouse. There's no real financial advice to be had here; you need to compromise until you're on the same page about what you ultimately want to achieve.

After that, you'll need to build your plan to get there. If your spouse hasn't ever really engaged in any financial planning, this can be a tough sell – he or she may just want to keep going without a plan. If you've been diligently saving, you may be able to be your own best example of why saving is important – revealing that you've been building up a large nest egg can be proof positive that simple financial planning is worthwhile. On the other hand, your spouse may see that as a windfall to be spent on vacations and luxuries. If you're this far apart, I recommend talking to a financial counselor. Whatever you do, just try to remind your spouse that your goal isn't just to be cheap now and hoard money for later, it's to ensure that for the rest of your lives together, money is a tool that lets you get what you need, not an object of great stress.

As the old rhyme says, first comes love, then comes marriage, then comes the baby in the baby carriage. Before you get to that last step, come up with a plan for your future child(ren). Before they're born (or conceived) is the best time to make some major decisions:

How many children do you plan to have?

Do one or both of you want to stay home full time to raise them?

Where do you plan to raise them?

Do you intend to send them to private or public schools?

Is it important to you that you pay for their college education?

These will give you an idea of how much income you'll need to have and whether or not the lifestyle you want is realistic. You may want to have five kids, send them all to private school and both stay home as full time parents, but unless you've already saved a lot and have assets that are generating income, that's probably just not possible. Better to figure it out now than after you've had child number five, since now you have more options today. You can have fewer children, one of you can continue working full time or you can send them to public school. If none of those sound appealing, now may be the time to start your own business so you can work from home after you have kids, thus providing income but also allowing you to be with them during the day.

If you do want to provide for your children's college education, I strongly recommend creating college funds for them as they're born. By putting away money up front, you gain a few things. First, you're giving yourself a way to have a meaningful, intelligent conversation about money with your kids as they think about college. If you just offer to pay for anyplace they want to go, they may not consider the cost of school or how their school and major will affect their ability to earn money later. If, on the other hand, they have a college fund with a set amount of money, they can consider financial tradeoffs – maybe it's better to take that full scholarship to their second choice school and leave with tens of thousands of dollars still available from their college fund. Beyond this, you'll help to ensure your future children don't end up as the Van Wilders of their schools – if the money to pay for school is going to run out, they're more liable to focus, study and graduate on time.

Before starting college funds, it's best to have a brief chat with a financial advisor. These types of funds are very common, but you want to make sure that you're setting them up correctly to ensure that you get all the tax benefits they provide.

You may also want to set some age at which each child gets the fund if it's not already spent (so your kid who picked his second choice school reaps the benefits of his good financial choices). In terms of the contents of the fund, I recommend the same investment that you have for yourself – an S&P ETF.

Unexpected windfalls

Whether it's a winning lottery ticket or an unexpected inheritance, finding yourself with some unexpected cash in hand is always a great feeling. With that great feeling, though, also comes the temptation to spend it. I'm not going to tell you not to – after all, if you're on track to retire without that money, then you won't get off track of you spend it. That said, I will encourage you to only spend some of it, and to spend it in a financially sound way. If it's a lot of money, use it as the down payment on a home (or buy the whole home in cash). That way you can have something amazing to show for it while also helping to build for your future.

That said, make sure you don't buy more house than you can afford – even if you get enough cash to buy a house outright, you'll still have to handle maintenance and taxes, so make sure you have enough income to take care of those.

Of course, it never hurts to save either – if you add as much of that windfall to your nest egg as possible, that just gives you the choice between retiring a little earlier than you would have otherwise, living a nice lifestyle in retirement or passing some of that money along to your children or favorite charity.

Chapter 19: Most Common Pitfalls When Trying To Follow A Budget

You have your budget and know how much you want to spend on each section. However, you always seem to go over each month and you aren't sure why. It's rare for anyone to perfectly stick to their budget. This chapter goes over some of the most common reasons why and how to respond

Pitfall #1: Not knowing exactly where your money is going each month

Doing the math on your budget isn't usually fun, so maybe when you wrote your budget, you didn't actually add up how much you spend. You just picked a number that looked good (i.e. $500 on groceries per month) and then realize you're always going over. Before you chose that number, did you add up how much you actually spend on groceries? A budget shouldn't be based on idealism and what you wish you were spending. It needs to reflect reality in all its gritty details. Even that coffee you buy should be counted, because eventually, all those coffees add up. If you don't put them into your initial number of what you spend each month, the budget you want to follow will be much tricker.

Solution: Keep track of everything you spend money on - coffees, grocery runs, movie tickets, bills, and more. This way, you'll be able to see where you're overspending and can make adjustments. Maybe you'll find that the number you picked for your groceries just isn't realistic based on what you need, so you decide to increase it. On the other hand, you might decide that you do want to stick closer to your budget goal, so you'll have to find ways to reduce your spending, which we'll get into in the next chapter. Whatever you decide, tracking your spending gave you the information necessary to make a change, and keeps you in control of your budget.

Pitfall #2: Not accounting for unexpected expenses

Every budget should be at least a little bit flexible, because life is unpredictable. Maybe you've allocated $40 per month for your pets, but then your dog eats a piece of chocolate and you take him to the vet. He's fine, but that appointment cost $80. If you budgeted every single dollar you make per month into your budget, even that extra $40 that puts you over will be a problem. Unexpected events happen all the time, whether it is your dog deciding to be stupid, or your car breaking down, or getting invited to a wedding and needing to buy a present. If your budget is too rigid, you'll always be overspending.

Solution: Build a cushion into your budget. Expect unexpected things to pop up. When creating your budget, add extra dollars to all the budget sections, or even create an entire section that's just for surprises. You'll feel much more prepared for life's unpredictability and less likely to end up in a situation where you simply don't have the money for something, and needing to make hard choices. If you don't use all the money in your "surprise" section, that's great! The smartest step would probably be to roll it over to the next month or put it away in your savings.

Pitfall #3: Having the exact same budget for every month or season

As you just learned, budgets need to be flexible because life is unpredictable and bad things happen. Budgets should also be flexible because not every month plays out the same, especially when it comes to special occasions and holidays. These are good things, but they still cost money. An example of a month-to-month difference could be November vs. December. If you celebrate Christmas, you'll be buying gifts and spending more money on food in December when friends and family come over. If your budget doesn't reflect that change, you'll be going over and starting the new year discouraged and frustrated.

Solution: Factor these seasons into your budget and be prepared to tweak if needed. Think about your year and events you know are coming up. Let's use the example of November and December again. You know your parents are coming for Christmas. Your grocery budget will most likely need to be larger for that month. Your November budget might also look different; maybe you decide to be stricter about certain sections, so you can save for those bigger expenses in December. When you plan for these different seasons, you can stick to your budget and feel at ease about your finances.

Pitfall #4: You are impatient

You're excited about finally getting your spending under control and saving money. However, it's been a few months, and you keep going over. You feel discouraged, frustrated, and confused. What are you doing wrong? Tweaking categories and moving money around doesn't seem to be working. Is budgeting just not right for you?

Solution: Everyone can have a budget and stick to it. It just takes time. Any kind of life change goes through a period of growing pains, and finances are no exception. In fact, it can take quite a while to get into the habit of fiscal responsibility and finding out what works best. All those adjustments you make with categories are part of the process; they are not a sign that you're doing budgeting "wrong." Be patient with yourself and don't expect the first months to go perfectly smoothly without any overspending. Instead, take the opportunity to examine your habits and where you tend to overspend, and use that information to improve your budgeting skills.

Pitfall #5: Budgeting stress you out

You do not like dealing with money. The idea of creating and sticking to a budget gives you anxiety. This results in rushing through the creation of a budget and not taking the time to adjust it as needed. You keep overspending, and you know it's because you aren't being vigilant about budging, but you just hate the process so much. Is this just how life is going to be?

Solution: Figure out why you hate budgeting. Is it because you feel it's confusing and complicated? Are you using a specific type of software or budgeting style, and you really don't like it? Budgeting does not have to be a grueling chore and there are so many ways to create and manage one, that even people who really don't like can find something that works for them. If you hate spreadsheets, don't use them. Consider a simple budgeting software or app (we'll get into them in a later chapter) or asking for help from an expert. While budgeting may give you anxiety, you probably also feel anxiety from not having complete control over your expenses. Luckily, it's possible to find a stress-free budgeting method that gives you peace of mind.

Chapter 20: Important Budget Considerations To Make It Effective

Creating a budget is the best way to take control of your finances. It allows you to manage your limited resources and ensures that they go to the right expenses. This is particularly useful if you are trying to get out of debt. You need to monitor your expenses so you can maximize your debt payments and achieve financial freedom.

However, not everyone knows how to create their budget. It is not as simple as identifying your income and expenses. You need to make sure that the right details are there to make your budget a success. If you are unable to follow your budget, then you will fail in the long run.

Most of the time, the problem lies with expenses. An income is easy to identify. An expense can prove to be a bit trickier because if you fail to include important factors, you may not be able to stick to it. To help you, here are some considerations that you need to look into while preparing your budget.

The reason for budgeting? You need to define why you need to budget in the first place. Is it to pay off your debts? If that is the case, you should make sure you include a debt payment fund. If it is to achieve financial freedom, you need to arrange your budget so it can lead you towards that goal. By identifying your goal, you get the motivation that will make the sacrifices easier to accomplish.

Rank your goals by importance. Most of the time, your budget is created to either help you get out of debt and save for a big purchase. There are times, however, wherein both are needed. Choose which is the priority at the moment. Usually, the debt is the priority but make sure that you allocate some funds to your savings as well. And if you have more than one debt, it is also a good idea to concentrate on one debt. That means paying the minimum on all the debts but putting extra funds on your priority. That will help you get out of that debt faster and thus experience a milestone in your quest for financial freedom.

Include your fun expenses and rank them. One of the mistakes that people make when creating a budget is to take the fun things out of their budget entirely. This is not advisable because that will make it very difficult to follow. Cut yourself some slack and leave room for the fun things in your life. Just ensure that you rank it according to priority and choose the more economical ways to enjoy them. For instance, renting a movie is more economical than going to the cinema.

Let the household decide on the budget. Unless you live alone, your budget should be a collaboration between the whole family. It is important for you to include them because in one way or another, the changes in your spending will affect everyone. Even your children and especially your spouse should know what the budget is. Identify areas that the whole family can save on. For instance, you can all contribute by packing your lunch to work or school. You can even come up with a family project that can help increase your income so you can fit in all of your expenses - even your debt payments.

The bottom line here is to create a budget that you can follow. No matter how great your budget looks on paper, it is nothing if you cannot apply it in real life.

Chapter 21: The Positivity Of Passive Income

A passive income is one that you receive when you are not directly or materially involved. An example of this kind of income is a rental property, where you receive a certain amount of money every month from the property yet you do not work on the property every day. This kind of income is also taxable, just the same with the non-passive income. Dividends and interests earned in some kind of investments are also considered passive income.

Passive income is quite beneficial in many ways. When you get a loss on a passive activity for instance, only the profits that you receive will be lost and not the income or initial investment as a whole. You may for instance not make income from an empty rental property but the property will still remain the same.

Here are some passive income ideas that one can consider in order to generate some personal income to boost personal finances:

Investing in eBooks

Creating an eBook can seem like a considerable amount of effort and work at the beginning, but once the tough part has been accomplished, you can always earn some passive income from it for a long time. EBooks can be sold on your website or you can partner with other websites that are selling the same content as what you have on the eBook. Just ensure that you create a good eBook and market it well and see how much revenue it can earn you for years.

Starting a lending club

People are always looking out for a loan lender especially for short term loans. You can be that lender that they will always turn to you whenever they need some financial backup, then you will be get some income from the interest you will be charging on the loans you issue out.

Real estate investment

Buying and improving a real estate property that you can always rent out or lease out is a great way to earn some passive income for several years. What you do is to keep it well managed and maintained and it can perform well for a very long time.

Affiliate marketing

This is another great way to earn some passive income for a while. What you do is to create a website through which you will be marketing products of certain companies that will pay you a certain amount of money or a commission after some sales have been done. Companies are always looking for avenues to market their products therefore you will never run short of clients this way.

Chapter 22: The Many Ways To Save Money

Budgeting is very similar to a ballroom dance – there is always a lead and a follow. In dance, the male dancer is considered the 'lead' and the female dancer is the 'follow' because she follows the directions signaled by the lead. In budgeting, the income should be the lead and expense the follow. That should be the ideal set-up for every household budget. Unfortunately, this is often not the way things work. Many people still choose to live beyond their means and, often, the outflow of cash is greater than the inflow. Reducing your expenses can help you to save money.

Are you fond of eating out? Too lazy or no time to cook? You might want to change your dining habits if you plan to buy that new car. Or if you want to have your house renovated, then it's time to stop ordering delivery or takeout. According to recent studies, the number of families that eat out has significantly increased in the last couple of years, more often than not, for the convenience of it due to lack of time. It seems people are too busy these days to have the time to plan for a meal and actually cook it. However, eating out all the time can create a big dent in the household budget. Cooking and eating in is simply more affordable, not to mention usually healthier.

You can enjoy a dramatic drop in your expenses by buying products in bulk, choosing on-sale items, and knowing where to shop for cheaper goods. Buy toilet paper as well as other products in large packs because the price in retail will typically cost less per roll that way. Look out for products that are on-sale. Many groceries and department stores offer discounted items once a month or on holidays. There are also 'buy one get one free' promos that you can take advantage of. Last, compare the prices of goods between grocery stores and always buy the products you need from the store that offers them for a more affordable price. If you want to have some savings in the bank, you cannot live extravagantly beyond your means. Since there are quality products that are available for more affordable costs, it only makes sense that these be the products that you buy. Don't live like a king while not having an emergency fund. It's better to live economically today and have a nest egg to look forward to tomorrow.

If you are really serious about saving money and cutting your expenses in half, then you should be willing to make certain sacrifices. These do not need to be huge. Stay within your budget but if you can actually minimize your expenditures, then why not do it? It can help you save more money and you become a step closer to achieving your financial goals.

Chapter 23: Grow Your Money

With experience, one shall become a pro in budgeting and financial planning. By keeping targets and inculcating discipline in your life, you shall slowly get rid of all your debts as well. The next question to ask is whether that is enough. Are you satisfied? No? Do you want your money to grow?

When I was young, most women used to be homemakers. They chose to be stay at home moms and played a huge role in upbringing the generation that forms the working youth of nations today. They did not have a major role in contributing to the finance of the domestic household; however, she performed the core role of making the house a home. She looked after every member's daily needs and nourishment. Her family would fall apart in her absence.

Today, apparently , it is harder to be a stay at home mom. It is less trendy now and with the rising prices, it is tougher to manage with a sole breadwinner. It requires more skills to make ends meet, than it did before. They are often education and smart women, who chose to stay back home to take care of a new addition to the family. However, along with managing your finances, you can also make tiny efforts to grow your money. Let us see how.

1) Save more, spend less - Having savings is the first step to growing. Once you cover all your debts, aim at saving. Cut back on what you do not really need. You need to save at every step possible, whether it is at the grocery store or making small changes in every arena. Brew your own coffee instead of grabbing one at Starbucks, focus on efficiently consuming what is there at home instead of ordering from out and similar such small steps that will lead to big savings

2)   Earn in your free time - Until your kids are infants, they need your complete attention. Perhaps, that would not leave you with much spare time. Nevertheless, as they grow they join pre-school and then get into regular schooling so in those years you may utilize that time into something productive. You may put in a couple of hours and make good money. There are various options available for a stay at home mom, to earn a few dollars. We may explore a few-

• Blogging- If you have a good command over your grammar and have good language skills, you may start blogging and make money from it. Regular posting is the key to a successful blog. You may put up ads to make money per click.

• Freelancing- this is flexible and provides wide opportunity. Simply make an account in any of the popular websites and pitch clients to get good work that suits you.

• Home skills- If you feel writing is not your forte, then you may invest any of your skills such as cooking, stitching, baking, teaching, art and craft etc. With these, you can provide services like catering, tailoring, delivering cakes for events, tutoring, or perhaps an online website selling goodies.

3)   Invest - Investment is asset appreciation. Investing your money will help you in the long term. However, you have to research and think well before making the right investments. A few pointers could be

● Broaden your horizons – risking everything on one endeavor is not a good idea. It is better to broaden your horizons and invest in different companies to reduce any peril if one company does not perform well.

● A step at a time- when you start with investing, take it slow and focus on growing gradually. Put some of your money in savings as well. Investment is a long-term plan, therefore begin with investing about sixty per cent and saving forty per cent. As you come closer to your retirement age, the savings would gradually increase and investment percentage decreases.

• Be wary of financial swindles- Very few investments are too good to be true. We have to be realistic about the returns. Therefore, make confident investments for long term that will grow over the time. Long-term investments do not get affected by fluctuations in the stock market.

• Make note of taxes- You may invest through a retirement account or traditional account. Both of them charge taxes during contribution but offer you to withdraw without any tax on your retirement.

• Stay motivated and read- Reading and being updated with business news is a must to understand your investments

• You house- Buying your house is a major investment. However, one needs to buy it in the right time when one plans to reside permanently at one location. If you do not intend to reside there permanently, it is wiser to rent a house.

Enticed by earning big amounts, many investors enter the field of stock market. Making money in the stock market is not so easy. However, with experience and prudent steps one may increase their chances of good returns. Consult with your spouse, take wise decisions in investment and keep yourself updated. It shall only be a matter of a few years when you will see your money channeled into a lot more systemic and productive stream.

Conclusion

Thank you again for downloading this book!

I hope this book was able to help you start following a budgeting system.

Your next task is to implement the plans stated in this book. You should keep on tracking your performance and look for areas where you can improve. Budgeting can only make a big impact in your life if you practice it consistently for a long time.

Given enough time, you will be able to reach your financial goals one at a time. After you reach all your short-term goals, you can start accumulating wealth for an early retirement and other long-term financial goals.

Thank you and good luck!